PURE VEGETARIAN
INDIAN COOKERY

PURE VEGETARIAN
INDIAN COOKERY

PURE VEGETARIAN INDIAN COOKERY

PRITAM UBEROI
&
NIMMI UBEROI

STERLING PUBLISHERS PRIVATE LIMITED

STERLING PUBLISHERS PRIVATE LIMITED
L-10, Green Park Extension, New Delhi-110016
Ph.: 6511784, 6511785 Fax: 91-11-6851028
E-mail: sterlin.gpvb@axcess.net.in

Pure Vegetarian Indian Cookery
©1992, Pritam Uberoi and Nimmi Uberoi
ISBN 81 207 1327 3
First Edition 1981
Reprint 1982, 1983, 1984, 1985, 1987, 1989, 1991
Second Revised Edition 1992
Reprint 1993, 1995, 1996, 1998

PRINTED IN INDIA

Published by Sterling Publishers Pvt. Ltd., New Delhi-110016.
Printed at Ram Printograph (India), Delhi-110051.

INTRODUCTION

For the last thirty-five years I have devoted myself to lecturing and teaching in colleges, and held many demonstrations in the art of cooking for charity programmes. At the request of my pupils and well-wishers, I have ventured on a task which I sincerely hope will be of material benefit, not only to Indian housewives but also to housewives abroad. Every recipe in this book can be used in any country by the ordinary housewife.

Vegetarian cakes and puddings, mentioned in this book, are my special innovations. My preparations of western dishes have also been admired by connoisseurs. My dishes were displayed at the 15th World Vegetarian Conference held at Delhi in 1957 which were highly appreciated by the press and the public.

It will not be out of place to mention here that my daughter Nimmi has rendered most invaluable assistance with her excellent professional expertise in cookery, as is immensely demonstrated in the compilation of this book, which task would have remained incomplete without her tacit help, given with such interest and perfection.

Not only this, but she has also given me most sincere and intimate support and help in organising a variety of cookery programmes, demonstrations and holding of regular classes for which I am ever so grateful to her. In fact I have drawn a great deal of inspiration from her unique contributions, which have left a vivid impact not only on my mind but also in this book as reflected throughout in the shape of numerable recipes covering all kinds of food and confectionery.

My family members have always provided constructive criticism of my culinary experiments. I am highly grateful to them. Finally, I also wish to thank all those who have encouraged me in writing the non-vegetarian and vegetarian cookbooks.

B-5/5, Safdarjang Enclave,   **Pritam Uberoi**
New Delhi-110029

CONTENTS

GLOSSARY

English	Hindustani
Almond	*Badam*
Alum	*Phitcari*
Aniseed	*Saunf*
Apricots	*Khurmani*
*Asafoetida	*Heeng*
Baking Powder	*Pakane Ka Soda*
Bay leaf	*Tej Patta*
Beans	*Same*
Beetroot	*Chukander*
Black Pepper	*Kali Mirchi*
Bottlegourd	*Lauki, Ghia*
Brinjal	*Baingan*
Buttermilk	*Lassi, Ghol*
Cabbage	*Band Gobhi*
Capsicum	*Simla Mirchi, Bara Mirchi*
Cardamom	*Elaichi*
Carrot	*Gajar*
Castor Sugar	*Powder or Pisi Cheenee*
Cashewnuts	*Kaju*
Caraway	*Ajwain*
Cayenne	*Lal Mirchi*
Cauliflower	*Phool Gobhi*
Chapati	*Indian Bread*
Cheese	*Vilayati Paneer*
Chillies	*Lal Mirchi*
Cinnamon	*Dalchini*

*Asafoetida water: Heeng water (mix one teaspoon ground hing into one cup hot water).

English	Hindustani
Citric acid	*Tatri*
Clarified Butter	*Butter Ghee*
Cloves	*Laung*
Cooking Apple	*Khatta Seb*
Cochineal	*Meetha Gulabi Rang*
Coconut	*Narial*
Colocasia	*Arbi*
Coriander Leaves	*Hara Dhania*
Coriander Seeds	*Sukha Dhania*
Cottage Cheese	*Paneer*
Cucumber	*Kheera*
Cuminseeds	*Jeera*
Curds	*Dahi*
Dates	*Khajur*
Drumsticks	*Saijan ki Phali, Singi*
Dried Ginger	*Sonth*
Dry Breadcrumbs	*Sookhi Double Roti ka Choora*
Fenugreek	*Methi*
Flour	*Maida*
French Beans	*Fras Beans*
Garlic	*Lahsoon*
Ghee	*Clarified Butter*
Ginger	*Adarak*
Gram	*Chana*
Gram Dal	*Chana ki Dal*
Gram Flour	*Besan*
Grapes	*Angoor*
Green Chilli	*Sabaj Mirch*
Griddle	*Tawa*
Groundnut Oil	*Moongphali Oil*
Guchhi	*Black Mushrooms*
Icing Sugar	*Icing Cheenee*
Jaggery	*Gur*

English	Hindustani
Kewara Flavour	Indian Kewara Essence diluted with Water
Khoya	Milk Solidified by Prolonged Cooking
Kulfi	Indian Icecream
Ladysfingers	Bhindi
Lemon	Neembu
Lemon Rind	Neembu ka Chhilka
Lentils	Dal
Mace	Jawitri
Macaroni	It is prepared from flour and made into various shapes
Mango	Aam
Mango Powder	Amchoor
Melon Seeds	Magaz
Mint	Pudina
Mustard	Rai, Sarson
Mustard Oil	Sarson Oil
Nutmeg	Jaiphal
Onion	Pyaz
Onion Seeds	Kalaunji
Papaya	Papita
Peas	Matar
Peppercorn	Sabut Kali Mirch
Peaches	Aadu
Pickle	Achar
Pistachio	Pista
Pomegranate Seeds	Anardana
Poppy Seeds	Khus Khus
Pressed Rice	Chewra
Raddish	Mooli
Raisins	Kismis
Red Chilli Powder	Kashmiri Mirch Powder
Rice	Chawal

English	Hindustani
Rose Water	*Gulab Jal*
Saffron	*Kesar*
Salt	*Namak*
Sesamum	*Til*
Semolina	*Sooji, Rawa*
Sevian	*Vermicelli*
Soda bicarbonate	*Meetha Soda*
Soft Breadcrumbs	*Taji Double Roti ka Choora*
Spinach	*Palak*
Spring Onion	*Hara Pyaz*
Sugar	*Cheenee*
Sultana	*Munakka (bara kismis)*
Sweet Potato	*Shakarkandi*
Tamarind	*Imli*
Turnip	*Shalgam*
Turmeric	*Haldi*
Thymol Seeds	*Ajwain*
Vermicelli	*Sevian*
Vinegar	*Sirka*
White Gram	*Kabuli Chana, White Chana*
White Mushrooms	*Dhingri*
White Pumpkin	*Petha*
Wholewheat Flour	*Gehun ka Atta*

IMPORTANT HINTS

Instead of ghee any kind of fat can be used such as dripping, hard margarine, suet or any edible oil.

Garlic powder can be used instead of fresh garlic. $1/4$ teaspoon garlic powder is equal to 4 garlic flakes.

Half tin spinach is equal to 2 pounds of fresh spinach.

1 teaspoon dry ginger is equal to 2 teaspoons fresh ginger (soak dry ginger powder in $1/4$ cup of water).

Curries should always be cooked slowly to extract all the richness and flavour of the spices.

Use soda bicarbonate for softening vegetables sparingly as it destroys the vitamins. Small amounts are often used in green vegetables to retain their colour.

Do not use large amount of water for cooking vegetables. Scrape the skins of vegetables, and do not peel them as Mrs Peeler is the Vitamin stealer.

Cook fleshy food on a low fire till tender. Excessive cooking destroys the food value.

COMPLEMENTARY RECIPES

PANEER

1 litre milk
2 tsps powdered citric acid
3 tsps oil or ghee

Put oil or ghee in the milk and boil. Remove from fire. Add 2 cups of water to milk. Dissolve citric acid in 1 cup of hot water and pour into the milk and put it on fire; cook till the milk curdles. Remove from fire, add more water to cool. Strain through a muslin cloth and put under weight for half an hour. Cut into cubes and deep fry till golden brown.

KHOYA

Grease a karahi, pour milk in it. Thicken on fire, stirring constantly with a flat spoon. Scrape the sides and the bottom of the karahi, taking care that the milk does not stick at the bottom. When the liquid becomes quite thick, remove from fire, gather into a lump and keep aside to cool. It will become solid after sometime and can be kept for a couple of days. One litre of full cream milk makes nearly 200 gms of khoya.

CARAMEL SYRUP

$^1/_2$ cup water
2 tsps sugar

Heat the sugar in a pan till it melts and gradually turns brown. Pour water over it and stir till it dissolves. Remove from fire; cool. It can be stored in a bottle for six months.

GROUND SPICES

1 cup cuminseeds
$^1/_2$ cup coriander seeds
$^1/_2$ cm piece cinnamon
6 big cardamoms
12 cloves

Grind all the spices together finely and store in an airtight jar.

SOUPS

CARROT CREAM SOUP   *serves 8*

340 gms chopped carrots
90 gms boiled rice
4 cups water
30 gms butter
3 tsps cornflour
1/2 tsp white pepper

1 spring onion
4 cups milk
1 tsp sugar
1 tsp chopped coriander
   leaves
salt to taste

Mix the cornflour to a smooth paste with a little milk. Boil the rest of the milk and stir in the cornflour paste and cook until it becomes a little thick. Keep aside. Cook the chopped carrots and onion in butter on very low fire for five minutes, being careful not to brown the carrots. Add the milk stock, boiled rice, salt, pepper, sugar, water and coriander, bring to boil and simmer, with lid on, for 35 to 40 minutes. Pass through a sieve, reheat and then remove from the fire and add 30 gms butter. Serve hot. (If carrot soup is too thick, mix a little milk with it.)

MIXED VEGETABLE SOUP—I   *serves 6*

6 cups water
2 medium onions, sliced
50 gms beans
1 clove
1/2 tsp salt
4 tsps grated cheese
white pepper to taste

4 small potatoes, cubed
2 carrots, diced
3 large tomatoes, skinned
2 tbsps split green peas
1/4 cup butter
4 tsps flour

1

Combine all the ingredients except the butter and cheese in a large soup pan, cover and boil gently till tender. Strain. Heat the butter, add the flour, fry for a few minutes without browning. Add strained soup and stir for five minutes. Remove from the fire, sprinkle with cheese and serve.

MIXED VEGETABLE SOUP—II   *serves 8*

2 carrots
1 potato
120 gms peas
60 gms butter
3 cups milk
3 tsps cornflour

1 big turnip
1 spring onion
2 tsps chopped coriander
   leaves
4 cups boiling water
salt and white pepper to
   taste

Melt the butter in a pan and fry the chopped vegetables and peas slowly on medium heat for 5 minutes. Then add water and salt and let it simmer till tender. Remove from the fire. Mix cornflour with milk and cook till a little thick. Pour it on cooked vegetables, stir and cook for a few minutes. Add salt, white pepper and serve hot.

PEA CREAM SOUP   *serves 6*

$1/_2$ kg green peas
salt, white pepper to taste
$1/_2$ tsp chopped mint
30 gms butter
$1/_4$ cup cream

4 cups water of pea pods
1 spring onion
5 gms arrowroot
1 cup milk
1 tsp chopped onion

Shell the peas and wash the pods several times. Put the pods in a pan, add water, salt and simmer gently for 35 minutes to extract their flavour and colour.

Strain the stock. Melt the butter, add onion and fry for one minute. Add the stock, peas, chopped spring onion and cook on low fire till the peas are tender. Pass through a sieve. Blend the arrowroot with milk and add to the soup, stirring all the time. At the time of serving, mix cream and chopped mint leaves lightly. Serve hot.

POTATO SOUP   *serves 6*

4 large potatoes	3 tbsps butter
2 spring onions	1 tbsp chopped coriander
$1/2$ tsp chopped ginger	leaves
1 cup tomato ketchup	2 carrots, diced
$1/4$ tsp white pepper	$1/2$ tsp salt
3 tbsps grated cheese	4 cups warm water

Boil the potatoes until soft; peel and pass through a sieve. Melt butter in soup pan, add chopped spring onions, coriander leaves, ginger and carrots and brown a little. Add tomato ketchup, salt, pepper, warm water and potatoes and simmer for 15 minutes. Serve with grated cheese.

LENTIL SOUP   *serves 8*

120 gms lentils	15 gms rice
9 cups hot water	1 large onion
1 large carrot	1 turnip
1 bay leaf	salt to taste
$1/2$ tsp white pepper	2 cloves
2 tsps chopped coriander	30 gms butter
leaves	$1 1/2$ tsps cornflour
$1/4$ inch piece cinnamon	croutons
1 cup milk	

3

Wash the lentils and rice with water. Chop the vegetables finely. Fry the vegetables and lentils in melted butter for five minutes. Add hot water, spices and salt. Bring to boil, cover the pan and simmer the vegetables till soft. Stir occasionally. Rub the ingredients through a sieve. Reheat the soup; blend the cornflour with milk, add to soup and cook for 7 minutes. Season well. Serve hot with croutons and coriander leaves sprinkled on it.

SPINACH CREAM SOUP serves 8

$^1/_2$ kg spinach	1 onion
30 gms butter	6 cups water
salt and white pepper to taste	5 gms cornflour
	$^1/_2$ cup cream
1 cup milk	croutons

Wash the spinach thoroughly. Slice the onion and fry in butter for a few minutes. Add the spinach and water and cook on low fire for 30 to 40 minutes. Pass through a sieve and add the arrowroot blended to a smooth paste with milk. Cook for 2 to 3 minutes, season to taste. Serve hot with croutons and cream mixed lightly in it.

TOMATO SOUP serves 6

$^1/_2$ kg tomatoes	4 cups water
1 medium carrot	1 onion
2 cloves	$^1/_2$ cm cinnamon
white pepper to taste	30 gms butter
$1^1/_2$ tsps pepper	cochineal colour
2 slices of fried bread	$2^1/_2$ tsps cornflour
2 tsps sugar	salt to taste

Cook whole tomatoes, whole spices with water, on low fire for 45 minutes. Rub through a wire sieve, return to the pan and cook. Blend the cornflour with stock or water, add to the soup and boil for 7 minutes. Mix sugar, salt and pepper, colour if necessary with cochineal. Serve hot with croutons. (Fried bread cubes)

TOMATO CREAM SOUP *serves 8*

1$^1/_2$ kgs tomatoes	**Cream**
2 onions	15 gms butter
2 bay leaves	3 tsps flour
salt to taste	$^1/_4$ tsp salt
3 cloves	$^1/_8$ tsp white pepper
2 tsps sugar	1 cup milk
water to cover the tomatoes	

Chop the onions. Put the tomatoes, chopped onions, bay leaves, salt, cloves with water in a pan and cook until tender and a little thick. Remove from the fire, cool and pass through a sieve. Heat the butter, fry flour in it till it is golden brown. Add the milk slowly, stirring constantly; cook till a little thick and smooth. Pass through a sieve and add salt and pepper. Heat the above strained tomato pulp and add the strained cream and mix it lightly. Serve hot with croutons.

Note: Do not heat the soup after mixing cream.

RICE AND PULAO

Savoury Pulaos

BOILED RICE
serves 6

$^1/_2$ kg rice   1 tsp salt
6 cups water

Pick, wash and soak the rice for 25 minutes. Boil the water with salt, add rice and mix well. Cover the vessel and cook on a low fire till the rice is cooked and water is absorbed and each grain is separate.

BASANT PULAO
serves 6

$^1/_2$ kg rice   1 tsp turmeric or $^1/_2$ tsp
4 cloves   yellow colour
5 cm piece cinnamon   6 cups water
salt to taste   1 tsp peppercorn
3 tsps cuminseeds   150 gms ghee

Pick, wash and soak the rice for 15 minutes. Heat the ghee and fry whole cinnamon and cardamoms for one minute. Add water and boil it. Now add turmeric or yellow colour, rice, salt and cuminseeds and peppercorns tied in a muslin bag. Cook in a vessel with a close-fitting lid, on medium fire, until tender and water is absorbed. Each grain of rice should be separate. Remove the muslin bag. Do not stir the pulao. Garnish with fried cashewnuts. Serve at lunch. (The pulao is served at Basant Panchami festival.)

CHANA DAL PULAO serves 6

$^1/_2$ kg rice
150 gms chana dal
1 tsp black peppercorns
1 onion, sliced
1 bay leaf
1 tsp black cuminseeds
150 gms ghee
6 cups water
$^1/_4$ tsp red chilli powder
4 cloves
2 cm piece cinnamon
2 big cardamoms
salt to taste

Soak the dal for 15 minutes and boil it in salted water until tender, and each grain is separate. Put in a strainer to remove excess water and keep aside. Fry the onion slices with bay leaf, cloves, cinnamon and cardamom until brown. Add water, rice, salt, peppercorns, red chilli powder and cuminseeds and cook on medium fire until tender and water is absorbed. Fry the boiled dal in 30 gms ghee for a few minutes and mix it lightly with cooked rice. Serve hot.

PANEER AND GUCHHI BIRIANI serves 6

$^1/_2$ kg rice
2 bay leaves
coarsely grind 4 cloves,
3 tsp white cuminseeds,
2 pieces cinnamon
4 green cardamoms
30 gms paneer, cubed
180 gms ghee
6 cups water
1 big onion
1 tsp red chilli powder
240 gms guchhi
4 silver leaves
2 tsps kewra flavour
1 carrot
2 tsps salt

Soak the guchhis in water overnight. Wash and soak the rice for one hour. Fry small pieces of paneer in ghee till light brown. Fry the chopped onion and bay leaves. Add water and salt and boil. Now add the rice, chopped carrot, and ground spices. Cook till water is absorbed and each grain is separate. Mix kewra flavour. Serve in an oval plate covered with silver leaves and fried cashewnuts. Serve hot.

Note: Tinned black mushrooms can be used instead of guchhis.

VEGETABLE BIRIANI   *serves 6*

Follow the above recipe, substitute mixed vegetables for guchhis.

FRIED RICE   *serves 6*

$1/_2$ kg rice	6 cups water
1 onion, sliced	2 bay leaves
1 carrot, sliced	$1^1/_2$ tsps chilli sauce
6 cloves powdered	2 green cardamoms
3 small pieces cinnamon	2 tsps white cuminseeds
240 gms peas	180 gms paneer, cubed
200 gms potatoes	2 green chillies
coriander leaves	$1/_2$ tsp ginger paste
2 tsps flour	4 tbsps ghee
2 tsps salt	salt to taste

Pick, wash and soak rice for 10 minutes. Deep fry paneer in ghee and keep aside. Fry the onion and bay leaf in ghee till brown. Add chilli sauce, salt, cloves, cardamoms, cinnamon, cuminseed powder and water and boil. Add the rice, carrot slices, peas and fried paneer pieces and cook until the rice has absorbed all the water and each grain is separate. Put fried balls of potatoes and cover the vessel.

Fried potato balls

Boil potatoes, cool and mash. Add chopped green chilli, salt, coriander leaves, and ground ginger and mix. Make round balls of potatoes, dust with flour and

8

dip in ground rice paste and fry in hot ghee till golden brown.

Rice paste

$^1/_2$ cup rice

Soak the rice and grind finely with water to form soft paste.

PEAS AND PANEER PULAO   serves 6

$^1/_2$ kg rice	6 cups water
$^1/_2$ kg shelled peas	120 gms paneer
2 onions, sliced	2 bay leaves
$^1/_2$ tsp red chilli powder	150 gms ghee
4 green cardamoms	2 small pieces of cinnamon
3 cloves	2 tsps white cumin powder
salt to taste	60 gms cashewnuts

Soak the rice for 15 minutes. Fry onion slices with bay leaves, cloves and cardamoms until brown. Add water, rice, red chilli powder, salt, cumin powder and paneer. Cook until tender and water is absorbed. Garnish with fried cashewnuts. Serve hot.

Paneer

$^1/_2$ litre buffalo's milk $^1/_2$ to $^3/_4$ tsp powdered citric acid

Boil the milk and remove from the fire. Add citric acid dissolved in one cup hot water gradually, until the milk curdles. Put it in a thick muslin cloth and squeeze out the water. Put under a weight for 30 minutes. Cut it into cubes and deep fry in ghee until golden brown.

MIXED VEGETABLE PULAO serves 6

Substitute carrots and potatoes for paneer.

POTATO KABAB PULAO serves 6

$^1/_2$ kg rice   6 cups water
$^1/_4$ cup red chilli powder $^1/_2$ teaspoon ginger paste
2 bay leaves   1 onion
2 tsps white cumin $^1/_4$ tsp cinnamon powder
   powder   salt to taste
2 powdered cloves

Wash and soak the rice for 15 minutes. Fry the onion slices with bay leaves until brown. Add water, rice, spices, ginger paste, red chilli powder and salt and cook on a medium fire until tender and water is absorbed. Remove from the fire. Put fried potato kababs on top and cover the vessel so that the kababs become a little soft. Serve hot.

Potato kabab

$^1/_2$ kg potatoes $^1/_2$ tsp fresh ginger,
2 green chillies   chopped
$^1/_2$ tsp black pepper   1 tsp chopped coriander
1 tsp cumin powder   leaves
30 gms flour for batter   salt to taste
ghee for deep frying

Boil the potatoes until tender. Peel and grate them. Mix ground cuminseeds, salt, black pepper, chopped ginger, coriander and chillies into mashed potatoes. Make small oval-shaped balls. Dust with flour and dip into flour batter. Fry in hot ghee until golden brown.

Sweet Pulaos

CARROT PULAO
serves 8

$^1/_2$ kg rice
300 gms sugar
6 cups water
2 tsps kewra flavour
3 silver leaves
15 gms pistachio

150 gms ghee
6 green cardamoms
$^1/_2$ kg grated carrot
30 gms raisins
$^1/_2$ tsp yellow colour

Put sugar, 1 cup water and grated carrots in a vessel and cook until half tender. Heat the ghee and fry soaked rice, cardamoms, 5 cups water and yellow colour and cook until water is evaporated. Now add the syrup prepared with $1^1/_2$ cup water and sugar, carrots and raisins and cook until rice is tender. Sprinkle kewra flavour and decorate with silver leaves and pistachios. If the rice is grainy, cover it with a wet cloth and cover the vessel tightly and keep on very low fire or over a pan of hot water for a couple of minutes. Serve hot.

KESARI PULAO
serves 8

$^1/_2$ kg rice
$^1/_2$ tsp orange colour
6 green cardamoms
$1^3/_4$ cups milk
60 gms raisins
15 gms pistachios
2 tsps kewra flavour

150 gms ghee
300 gms sugar
4 cloves
$4^1/_2$ cups water
60 gms almond
$^1/_4$ tsp kesar
4 silver leaves

Wash and soak the rice for 25 minutes. Heat sugar and 1 cup water in a vessel until syrupy. Heat the ghee with cloves and cardamoms, add rice, orange colour, water and cook on a low fire until water is evaporated. Now add the milk, syrup and kesar dissolved in a little water. Cook on a very low fire until the rice is tender and each grain is separate. Mix blanched almonds (slit in halves), raisins, and pistachio slices with rice and cover the vessel. Sprinkle kewra flavour and decorate with silver leaves. Serve hot.

MANGO PULAO
serves 8

¹/₂ kg rice	60 gms almonds and
1 cup ripe mango pulp	pistachios
110 gms ghee	240 gms castor sugar
6 green cardamoms	2 tsps kewra flavour
60 gms cashewnuts and raisins	

Heat the ghee and add soaked rice, cardamoms, 5 cups water and mango pulp and cook on a low fire, until tender and water is absorbed. Transfer into another vessel and mix with castor sugar and kewra flavour lightly. Spread on an oval plate. Decorate with silver leaves, blanched almonds and pistachio slices and serve hot.

SHAHI SWEET PULAO
serves 8

¹/₂ kg rice	120 gms ghee
6 cups water	250 gms sugar
30 gms cherries	30 gms almonds
15 gms raisins	15 gms pistachios
6 silver leaves	6 green cardamoms
150 gms khoya	3 tbsps castor sugar
¹/₂ tsp kewra flavour	

¹/₂ tsp of each colour: orange, green, red and yellow

Pick, wash and soak rice for 25 minutes. Make a syrup of sugar with one cup of water. Remove from the fire and keep aside. Heat the ghee, add crushed green cardamoms, rice and water. When the water is absorbed, add the syrup. Simmer until the rice is tender and the syrup has been absorbed; pour each colour separately on the rice. Let the rice remain on fire for 2 minutes. Remove from the fire, add khoya mixed with castor sugar and kewra, mix well with rice and keep it covered. Chop cherries, almonds and pistachios for decoration. Spread the rice in an oval plate. Decorate with silver leaves, almonds, pistachios and cherries. Serve hot.

RAINBOW FRUIT PULAO serves 8

$1/_2$ kg rice
6 cups water
60 gms dessicated
  coconut
60 gms pistachios
8 green cardamoms
5 silver leaves
$1/_4$ tsp of each colour:

250 gms sugar
120 gms sultanas
120 gms blanched
  almonds
30 gm cherries
2 tsp kewra flavour
120 gms khoya

  green, red, yellow and orange colours

Make a thin syrup of sugar and one cup water and keep aside. Heat the ghee with cardamoms, then add soaked and drained rice and water and cook until water is absorbed. Add the syrup, mashed khoya, fried sultanas, coconut and almonds and keep it on very low fire until the rice is cooked. Now pour each colour on the rice and cover the vessel with a close-fitting lid. Remove from the fire. Serve pulao in an oval dish, decorated with silver leaves, pistachios and cherry slices. Serve hot.

PARATHA, PURI AND NAN

Paratha

CHAPATI   *serves 6*

$^1/_2$ kg wholewheat flour $^1/_2$ tsp salt
water to make the dough

Sift flour and mix with salt. Add enough water gradually to make a soft, but not sticky dough. Knead well, cover with a wet cloth and keep aside for an hour. Knead it again. Form into small balls and roll out into flat, round, fairly thin rounds. Bake on a hot griddle for a few seconds on each side. Place directly on hot charcoals or gas flame and puff it. Place on a napkin. Serve hot at lunch or dinner. Chapatis and plain parathas are eaten with dal, curry or bhujia (dry vegetables) at meals.

PLAIN PARATHA   *serves 10*

1 kg wholewheat flour   1 tsp salt
200 gms ghee

Sift the flour, add salt and 1 tbsp ghee. Rub the ingredients between the palms to mix them thoroughly. Pour a little water at a time and knead to a soft but not too soft dough. Take a small portion of the dough, roll out into a chapati and smear with ghee. Fold up again into a round ball and roll out once more. Put one paratha at a time on a heavy and hot

14

griddle, bake one side and turn over. Add a little ghee from the sides till it gets a nice brown colour. Cook on a low fire and when ready, it should be crisp. Similarly, make more parathas. Serve hot.

BESAN PARATHA   *serves 8*

$^1/_2$ kg wholewheat flour	250 gms besan
salt to taste	$^1/_2$ tsp red chilli powder
125 gms ghee	1 tsp coarsely powdered
1 tsp chopped green	coriander seeds
chillies	2 tsps pomegranate seeds

Sift both the flours and knead them together with water into a dough as for chapatis. Mix all the above ingredients with the dough except the ghee. Make 12 round balls. Roll out each to a thick round, smear with a little ghee and fold it up again into a round ball. Dip the ball into dry wheat flour and roll out into a thin round paratha. Cook both sides of the paratha on a griddle and then baste well with ghee. Fry till golden brown on both sides. Serve hot at breakfast. Besan paratha is also served with curd at lunch.

CAULIFLOWER PARATHA   *serves 6*

$^1/_2$ kg wholewheat flour	1 big cauliflower
salt to taste	2 tsps coarsely powdered
120 gms ghee	coriander seeds
$^1/_2$ tsp red chilli powder	2 tsps pomegranate seeds
$^1/_2$ tsp black pepper	

Cut the cauliflower into small pieces. Discard the lower hard stalks, keep only the upper flower portions. Put them in a vessel with a little ghee, coriander, chilli powder, black pepper, pomegranate seeds and salt. Cook till the water is absorbed and the cauliflower is soft. Fry for a few more minutes, remove from the fire and when slightly cool, grind to a coarse paste. Knead the flour with a little salt to a smooth dough. Take two small portions of the dough, and roll out two equal chapatis. Cover one with a thin layer of the filling (paste) and smear the other with ghee. Place this over the other, join the edges and roll out into a round. Fry as ordinary parathas. Serve hot with plain curd.

Variation: The filling can also be prepared as follows:

Wash and dry the cauliflower and grate it. Squeeze out the water and mix with salt, ground spices, red chilli, black pepper, coriander leaves and pomegranate seeds. A variety of parathas can be prepared by varying the fillings. Some of them are given below:

CHANA DAL PARATHA   *serves 6*

250 gms chana dal
1 tsp chopped green
   chillies
salt to taste

2 tsps chopped coriander
   leaves
1 small chopped onion
2 tsps chopped fresh
   ginger

Pick, wash and soak chana dal for 15 minutes. Boil water, add chana dal and salt and cook until tender and each grain is separate. Strain to remove extra water. Cool and mix with all the above ingredients. Fill in the parathas (The dal water may be used to prepare the dough.)

METHI PARATHA serves 6

250 gms fresh methi
   leaves
salt to taste
125 gms ghee

1 tsp pomegranate
   seeds
$^1/_2$ tsp red chilli powder

Discard the stems of fenugreek and wash. Chop
finely. Sprinkle salt and keep aside for 10 minutes.
Squeeze out the water and mix with red chilli powder
and pomegranate seeds.

PEAS OR MATAR PARATHA serves 6

$^1/_2$ kg green peas
1 tsp ground spices
120 gms ghee

2 tsps coriander powder
salt and chilli powder to
   taste

Shell the peas, put in a vessel with water and salt,
cover and simmer on a low fire till soft. Drain and
grind the peas with ground spices, coriander and
chillies to a fine paste.

HARA CHANA serves 6

Omit peas, instead use fresh green gram.

PEETHI PARATHA serves 6

200 gms ground urad dal
   without husk
2 chopped green chillies
2 tsps ground spices
1 tbsp ghee

2 tsps chopped coriander
   leaves
$^1/_2$ tsp coarsely powdered
   coriander seeds
salt to taste

Mix all the above ingredients together and fry in ghee
on a low fire for 10 minutes. Cool and fill in parathas.

POTATO PARATHA
serves 6

500 gms boiled potatoes
2 tsps chopped green
  chillies
$1/_3$ tsp black pepper
2 tsps pomegranate seeds

2 tsps chopped coriander
  leaves
salt to taste
$1/_4$ tsp red chilli powder
120 gms ghee

Mash boiled potatoes and mix with all the spices and chopped ingredients.

RADISH PARATHA
serves 6

250 gms white tender
  radish
1 tsp coarsely powdered
  coriander
2 chopped green chillies

$1/_2$ tsp turmeric
salt to taste
$1/_2$ tsp red chilli powder
120 gms ghee
1 tsp pomegranate seeds

Grate and squeeze out all the water of the radish. Heat half of the ghee and fry grated radish with all the spices, salt, green chillies until dry, cool.

THYMOL SEED PARATHA
serves 6

Add 1 teaspoon thymol seeds to the dough.

Puri

ATTA KI PURI
serves 7

$1/_2$ kg wholewheat flour
$1/_2$ tsp salt
ghee for deep frying

50 gms ghee
water

Sift the flour and salt and knead it with water to a smooth and slightly stiff dough. Cover with a wet cloth and keep for one hour. Knead again and make small round balls about the size of a walnut. Roll out each ball into a round 1/2 mm thick and put in hot ghee. Press it until it puffs up and then turn it once, fry till light brown. Serve hot with any vegetable bhujia.

Variation: Omit wholewheat flour and use refined flour instead.

MALAI PURI   *serves 6*

250 gms flour $^1/_4$ cup cream
$^3/_4$ cup milk   250 gms potatoes
ghee for deep frying

Boil the potatoes, peel and mash to a smooth paste. Mix together flour, cream, mashed potatoes and a little salt thoroughly. Sprinkle a little milk and knead into a smooth and fairly stiff dough. Divide into small balls and roll out into thick puris. Heat enough ghee in a heavy frying pan and when smoking hot, reduce the fire and fry the puris golden brown on both sides. Serve hot with potato bhujia.

STUFFED POTATO PURI   *serves 6*

$^1/_2$ kg flour $^1/_2$ tsp salt
1 tbsp ghee   ghee for deep frying
$^1/_2$ kg potatoes   30 gms ghee
1 tsp white cuminseeds $^1/_2$ tsp red chilli powder
2 tsps ground spices   salt to taste
water

Boil the potatoes until tender. Cool and mash. Add all the spices, red chilli powder and salt to taste. Heat the ghee, add potatoes with spices and cook for a minute. Cool. Knead the flour into a dough as for atta puri. Make round balls, the size of billiard balls. Fill

19

mashed potatoes in each ball and roll them out into 1mm thick rounds. Deep fry in ghee until golden brown and puffed up. Drain to remove excess ghee. Serve hot at breakfast.

STUFFED PEETHI PURI serves 6

Omit potatoes and add 200 gms peethi instead.

Dosa, Nan, Batura

DOSA (SOUTH INDIAN) serves 6

400 gms rice	200 gms urad dal
1/2 tsp turmeric	1 kg potatoes
1 cup shelled peas	200 gms onion
2 tsps chopped coriander leaves	1 1/2 tsps mustard seeds
	50 gms green chillies
1 tbsp ghee	2 tsps chopped ginger
salt to taste	1 cup water

Soak the rice and dal separately overnight. Strain and grind them separately with the same water in which they were soaked. Mix the two together, add water to make a batter of thick consistency (pakora batter).

Filling

Heat the ghee, add mustard seeds. When they splutter, add chopped onion, peas and one cup water and cook until tender. Now add coarsely mashed boiled potatoes, chopped green chillies, ginger, coriander leaves and salt and mix well. Cook for two minutes. Cool. Heat a little ghee, then pour the batter on a griddle like a pancake and pour a little ghee round it. Fry one side until light brown. Put potato mixture on the dosa and fold over and serve.

NAN

350 gms flour
4¹/₂ tsps sugar
150 gm curds
6 tsps melted ghee
2 tsps poppy seeds

125 gms wholewheat flour
1 tsp salt
1¹/₄ tsps soda bicarbonate
2 tsp aniseed
¹/₂ tsp onion seeds

Sift the flour and wholewheat flour, mix with it salt, sugar, ghee and curds. Knead it with a little water until smooth and elastic. Keep it for 15 minutes. Meanwhile, heat the tandoor. Dissolve soda in ¹/₂ tbsp water and mix with the dough and knead it again. Make big round balls, flatten each between the palms of hands. Mix aniseed, onion seeds and poppy seeds in a little water and sprinkle over the nans. Flatten more with hands and then stretch lengthwise from the bottom and bake in a moderate tandoor. Cover the tandoor and leave the nan in it till golden in colour. Remove from the tandoor and serve hot. If it cannot be served immediately, wrap in a duster and keep in a covered vessel so that it remains soft.

BHATURA
serves 10

¹/₂ kg flour
100 gms yeast
ghee for frying

250 gms semolina
100 gms ground urad dal

Soak the semolina in 1¹/₂ cups of water, overnight. Add the soaked semolina and yeast into the sifted flour and knead it by adding a little warm water, until soft. Grease a metal dish with oil, put the dough on it and then sprinkle a little oil on it and keep for ¹/₂ hour. Now make round balls of the dough, fill urad dal mixed with a little salt and red chilli in each. Put on a greased metal dish and then sprinkle oil and keep for another half an hour. Flatten with palms of hands and deep fry in ghee till it puffs up. Turn over, fry till light brown.

Yeast

100 gms flour $1/4$ tsp soda bicarbonate
1 cup hot water   50 gms curd

Mix all the ingredients together and keep for one day in a warm place.

CURRIES

ARBI CURRY

serves 10

1 kg arbi	1 lemon
1¹/₂ tsps red chilli powder	2 tsps ground fresh ginger
1 cup curd	1 cup water
250 gms ghee'	1 tsp white cumin powder
salt to taste	2 tsps ground spices
1 tsp black pepper	

Peel and wash the arbi and prick it with a fork. Sprinkle with lemon juice and 1 tsp salt and keep it aside for one hour. Fry it in hot ghee until golden brown. Now mix turmeric, ground ginger, ground spices, red chilli powder, black pepper, ground white cuminseeds and salt with it. Stir it for a few minutes. Beat the curds with water, pour onto the fried arbi and cook until the gravy is thick. Remove from the fire. Sprinkle chopped coriander leaves. Serve hot.

CHANA DAL CURRY

serves 8

Curry

250 gms chana dal without husk	¹/₂ kg sour curds
15 cups water	1 tsp red chilli powder
2 tsps coriander powder	2 tsps ground spices
a small piece of asafoetida	1 tsp turmeric
1 tsp pomegranate seeds	¹/₂ cup ghee
	salt to taste

Soak 500 gms chana dal overnight. Drain and grind it finely. Divide the ground dal into two portions. Heat

23

the ghee, fry asafoetida until brown and crush it with a spoon. Fry half the dal with turmeric for 10 minutes. Add the curds beaten with water and stir it until it boils. Add pakoras, all the spices, salt and red chilli powder and cook on a low fire until thick, and pakoras become soft. Sprinkle coriander and serve hot with rice or chapatis. (Make it thick for serving with chapatis and thin for rice.)

Pakora

250 gms chana dal	1 tsp ground red chilli
1 tsp chopped fresh ginger	1 tsp chopped coriander
1 tsp chopped onion	1 tsp chopped green chilli
1 tsp ground spices	1 tsp coarsely powdered
ghee for deep frying	coriander seeds
salt to taste	

Now, with the other portion of the ground chana dal, mix all the above ingredients of pakoras. Heat the ghee, drop the mixture with a teaspoon or hand and fry the pakoras until brown. Drain and keep aside.

CREAM BALL CURRY serves 10

Curry

4 onions	5 cloves garlic
2 tsp ground fresh ginger	$1/_2$ tsp turmeric
200 gms tomatoes	few coriander leaves
1 tsp red chilli powder	2 tsps ground spices
3 tbsps ghee	1 tsp white cumin powder
salt to taste	

Fry the chopped onion and garlic till light brown. Add blanched and chopped tomatoes, ground ginger, turmeric, red chilli powder, salt and ground spices and stir until the gravy becomes thick. Add water and cook for 15 minutes.

Balls

2 litres milk	2 tsps citric acid
5 gms almond	5 gms pistachio
10 green cardamoms	ghee for deep frying

Boil the milk, dissolve citric acid in half cup of water and add gradually to milk until it curdles. Leave it for a few minutes to set. Strain through a muslin cloth and squeeze out all the liquid. Place the paneer on a clean thali or plate and knead it with one hand until it becomes soft. Grind almonds, pistachio nuts and green cardamoms with milk. Make round balls of paneer and in the centre of each ball, fill the ground almond, pistachio and cardamom mixture. Deep fry in ghee till golden brown. Put in the gravy and cook till soft. Serve hot.

CREAM KOFTA CURRY   *serves 10*

Kofta

7 plantains (raw bananas)	2 tsps salt
$1^1/_2$ tsps turmeric (for boiling bananas)	2 tsps ground fresh ginger
	3 tsps chopped coriander leaves
6 tsps dry breadcrumbs	
$1/_4$ tsp nutmeg	125 gms khoya
10 peeled almonds	4 green cardamoms
$1/_2$ tsp ground spices	

Cut the plantains into four pieces without peeling. Mix turmeric and salt in water and boil the pieces in it until tender. Cool, peel and mash and mix with chopped coriander leaves, ginger, breadcrumbs, salt and ground spices. To the khoya, add ground nutmeg, green cardamoms, almonds and a little mixture of mashed plantains. Make small balls of the khoya mixture and fill in each ball, a little plantain mixture

25

and shape them into koftas. Dust with flour. Fry in ghee until brown in colour.

Gravy

250 gms onion	12 cloves garlic
small pieces of coconut	3 tsp ground fresh ginger
1 tsp turmeric	60 gms tomatoes
2 tsps chopped coriander leaves	1½ tsps red chilli powder crushed green cardamoms
4 tsps ground spices	5 tbsps ghee
salt to taste	2 tsps white cuminseeds

Fry the chopped onion and garlic till light brown. Add salt, red chilli powder and cook till onions are brown. Add chopped tomatoes, ground ginger, ground coconut, ground white cuminseeds and ground spices and stir until it becomes a thick gravy. Add 3 cups of water and cook for 15 minutes. Now add fried koftas and cook until they are soft. Sprinkle chopped coriander leaves. Serve hot.

CHANA AND DHINGRI CURRY   serves 7

250 gms kabuli chana	60 gms dhingri
½ tsp turmeric	½ tsp red chilli powder
½ tsp black pepper	2 tsps chopped coriander leaves
2 tsps ground spices	
200 gms onion	200 gms tomatoes, skinned
1 ground garlic clove	
salt to taste	1 tsp ground fresh ginger
½ cup ghee	

Soak white mushroom and chana separately overnight. Cut mushrooms into small pieces. Boil the chana in salted water till tender. Heat the ghee, fry chopped onion until light brown, add ground garlic, ginger and $^1/_2$ cup water. To this, add chopped tomatoes, turmeric, red chilli powder and salt and stir till onion is tender. Now add the boiled chana and mushrooms and 1 litre of water and cook on a low fire until gravy is thick. Mix coriander and ground spices with it. Serve hot.

KHOYA MATAR CURRY   serves 8

250 gms khoya	1 kg peas
200 gms tomatoes	$^1/_2$ cup ghee
salt to taste	1 tsp asafoetida water
2 tsps white cumin powder	1 tsp red chilli powder
2 tsps ground spices	2 tsps chopped coriander leaves
$^1/_2$ tsp turmeric	1 tsp ground fresh ginger
30 gms gresh coconut	

Heat the ghee. Put asafoetida water in it, add the khoya and stir with a flat spoon until it is light brown. Add the peas, red chilli powder, ground white cuminseeds, turmeric, ground ginger, salt, ground coconut and water and cover the vessel. Fry the tomatoes in a frying pan and mix them with khoya and matar. Let it simmer for a few minutes until peas are tender. Put the ground spices with chopped coriander leaves. Serve hot.

MALAI KOFTA CURRY   serves 8

Kofta

$^1/_2$ kg potatoes	2 green chillies, finely chopped
$^1/_2$ tsp coriander leaves	
1 tsp cumin powder	1 tsp very finely chopped fresh ginger
$^1/_3$ tsp ground spices	

flour for batter (mix
  1/2 cup water with
  1/3 cup flour)
1/2 cup cream or malai

breadcrumbs for coating
ghee for frying
salt to taste

Boil the potatoes with 1 tsp salt till they become tender. Drain, cool, peel and grate them. Add ground spices, cuminseeds, coriander leaves, green chillies, ginger and salt and mix well. Make round flat balls and fill the malai or cream in each. Make round balls, and dip into flour batter. Coat with breadcrumbs and fry 3 or 4 at a time in hot ghee till golden brown.

Gravy

1 heaped cup chopped
  onion
2 tsps ground fresh ginger
1 tsp kasturi methi
1 tsp ghee
1 bay leaf
2 tsps cumin powder

4 cloves garlic
1 tsp red chilli powder
1 tbsp ground spices
250 gms tomatoes
4 green cardamoms
few coriander leaves
salt to taste

Fry the onion till light brown. Add ground ginger, garlic and 1 1/2 cups water and cook till the water is evaporated. Add bay leaf, chopped tomatoes, ground cuminseeds, ground spices, red chilli powder, green cardamoms, salt to taste and kasturi methi. Cook till the masala leaves its ghee. Then add 2 1/2 cups water and cook till 3/4 cup is left. Remove from the fire. Put the koftas in the dish and pour boiling gravy over this. Sprinkle chopped coriander leaves.

MUGLAI POTATO KOFTA CURRY *serves 8*

Kofta

1/2 kg potatoes
1 tsp ground fresh ginger
2 tsps green chillies

2 tsps ground poppy seeds
2 tsps chopped coriander
  leaves

1$\frac{1}{2}$ tsps cumin powder   1 tsp ground spices
salt to taste   4 green cardamoms
batter for dipping   breadcrumbs for coating
ghee for frying

Boil the potatoes in salted water till tender. Cool, peel and grate them, and mix with the above ground ingredients.

Filling

200 gms paneer $\frac{1}{2}$ tsp yellow colour
salt to taste

Mash the paneer and mix yellow colour and salt with it. Make round balls and cover with the potato mixture. Dip into the flour batter and coat with breadcrumbs and fry in hot ghee till light brown. At the time of serving, cut each kofta into half, pour the gravy in a dish and put the halved koftas in it.

Gravy

1 cup chopped onion   2 tsps ground ginger
6 cloves garlic   1$\frac{1}{2}$ tsps red chilli powder
1$\frac{1}{2}$ tsps cumin powder   2 tsps ground spices
4 green cardamoms   2 tsps ground poppy seeds
300 gms tomato   1 tsp coriander leaves
1 tsp sugar   1 tbsp ghee
salt to taste

Fry the chopped onion till light brown. Then add ground garlic, ginger, 1 cup water, red chilli powder and salt and stir till water is evaporated. Add blanched and chopped tomatoes, sugar, ground spices, cumin powder, crushed cardamoms and poppy seeds and stir till the mixture leaves its ghee. Now add 2 cups of water and cook till gravy is thick. Pour in a dish and decorate with koftas. Garnish with coriander leaves.

MINCED MUSHROOM CURRY   *serves 8*

120 gms white
  mushrooms
8 cloves garlic
2 tsps ginger
$1^1/_2$ tsps red chilli powder
1/2 kg peas
3 tbsps ghee
$1^1/_2$ tsps white cumin powder

4 onions
4 medium tomatoes
a few coriander leaves
2 tsps ground spices
3 green cardamoms
$^1/_2$ tsp turmeric
salt to taste

Soak white mushrooms overnight in water. Wash and mince them. Fry chopped onion, garlic until brown, add chopped tomatoes, ground ginger, turmeric, red chilli powder, salt, ground spices, crushed green cardamoms and white cumin powder and stir constantly until gravy becomes thick. Add minced mushrooms, peas and chopped coriander leaves and fry for two minutes. Add water and cook on a low fire until tender.

MUKUND VARI CURRY   *serves 6*

1 kg wholewheat flour
1 tsp salt
6 cloves garlic
2 tsps fresh ginger
1 tsp red chilli powder
2 tsps ground spices
  (cloves, cuminseeds,
  coriander seeds and cinnamon)

$^1/_2$ tsp turmeric
4 onions
2 tomatoes
a few coriander leaves
$^1/_2$ kg peas
3 tbsps ghee
salt to taste

Knead the flour as for chapatis and keep it aside for 15 minutes. Wash it several times in running water until it becomes elastic. Boil water with one tsp salt and add the elastic atta and cook until it increases to twice its volume. Remove from the water and cool.

Squeeze out the water and cut into small pieces. Fry in ghee till light brown.

Fry chopped onion and garlic in ghee until brown; add chopped tomatoes, ground ginger, turmeric, red chilli powder, salt and ground spices and stir constantly until done. Add peas, fried elastic atta and chopped coriander leaves, and fry for two minutes. Add 3 cups water and cook on a low fire until tender and one cup of water is left. Serve hot.

PANEER MATAR CURRY serves 8

Curry

750 gms peas	250 gms paneer
4 medium onions	6 small slices of fresh
10 cloves garlic	ginger
1 tsp red chilli powder	3 medium tomatoes
2 tsps ground spices	$^1/_2$ tsp turmeric
$^1/_2$ cup ghee	1 tsp chopped coriander
salt to taste	leaves

Heat the ghee, fry ground onion and garlic until light brown. Add $^1/_2$ cup water, fry ground ginger, chopped tomatoes, salt, turmeric and red chilli powder and stir for a few minutes. Put shelled peas and fried paneer pieces and saute for five minutes, then add 3 cups of water and cook until peas are tender. Mix ground spices and chopped coriander leaves. Serve hot.

POTATO CURRY serves 8

$^1/_2$ kg potatoes	120 gms onion
200 gms tomatoes	1 tsp fresh ginger paste
$^1/_2$ tsp garlic paste	1 tsp dry methi
$^1/_2$ tsp turmeric	1 tsp red chilli powder

1 tsp chopped coriander leaves
2 tsps ground spices
salt to taste
$^1/_2$ cup ghee

Fry chopped onion until light brown, add ground ginger, garlic, red chilli powder and turmeric and fry for a few minutes Add one cup of water and salt and stir for a minute, until onion is tender. Add peeled and chopped tomatoes and cook until a thin gravy is formed. Add potatoes, peeled and cut into big pieces, methi and fry for 10 minutes. Add 3 cups more water and cook on a low fire until tender. Remove from the fire and sprinkle chopped coriander leaves. Serve hot.

PUMPKIN KOFTA CURRY   serves 6

Kofta

1 kg pumpkin
2 tsps ground fresh ginger
2 ground green chillies
1 tsp ground spices
60 gms khoya
5 blanched almonds
30 gms flour for batter

6 tsps roasted besan or 6 tsp breadcrumbs
2 tsps chopped coriander leaves
$^1/_4$ cup cream
4 green cardamom
salt to taste

Grate the pumpkin and boil until tender. Squeeze out the water and add ground ginger, coriander leaves, green chillies, roasted besan or breadcrumbs, ground spices and salt and mix well. Make a paste of cream, khoya, ground almonds and green cardamoms. Make 12 round balls of cooked pumpkin, fill cream paste in each. Make a batter with flour and water, dip koftas into it and deep fry in ghee until brown.

Gravy

250 gms onion
2 tsps fresh ginger paste

6 cloves garlic
1 tsp turmeric

350 gms tomatoes
2¹/₂ tsps red chilli powder
5 tbsps ghee
2 tsps white cumin
  powder
4 green cardamoms, powdered

2 tsps chopped coriander
  leaves
4 tsps ground spices
¹/₂ cup khoya
salt to taste

Fry ground or chopped onion and garlic until light brown, add salt and water and cook till onion is tender. Add chopped tomatoes, ginger paste, red chilli powder, ground spices, white cuminseeds, cardamom powder and coriander leaves and stir until it becomes a thick gravy; add khoya and stir for a few minutes. Add water and cook for 15 minutes. Remove from the fire, put fried koftas in the gravy and keep for a few minutes and serve.

PUNJABI BESAN CURRY   serves 6

Curry

¹/₂ kg sour curds
1¹/₂ tsps coriander
  powder
¹/₄ cup ghee
1 tsp turmeric
1 tsp chopped coriander leaves

120 gms besan
1¹/₂ litres water
1 tsp pomegranate seed
³/₄ tsp red chilli powder
salt to taste

Beat the curds and mix besan with a wooden spoon. Add salt, dry coriander, red chilli and 1 litre water. Boil ¹/₂ litre water with turmeric. Pour besan mixture into it and stir constantly until it boils. Add ghee and continue boiling for 15 minutes, then add pakoras and cook until thick. Sprinkle coriander leaves. Serve hot with boiled rice or chapatis. (Keep the curds for 12 hours to make it sour.)

Pakora

120 gms besan	1 big onion
$1/4$ tsp red chilli powder	salt to taste
water	ghee for deep frying

Sift besan, add water gradually until a thick dropping consistency is formed. Mix salt, chilli powder and onion slices with it. Heat ghee well and put spoonsful of this mixture into it. Fry until golden brown, keep aside.

PANEER KOFTA CURRY   serves 6

Kofta

300 gms paneer	12 tsps arrowroot
5 tsps breadcrumbs	1 tsp ground spices
$1/4$ tsp soda bicarbonate	salt to taste

Filling

4 green cardamoms	4 tsps ground pistachios
15 ground almonds	$3/4$ cup paneer
$1/2$ tsp cumin powder	1 tsp ground spices
$1/4$ tsp yellow colour	ghee for frying

Mix the paneer, arrowroot, salt and spices and rub it till smooth. Mix soda bicarbonate, breadcrumbs and arrowroot with it. Make round balls. Mix all the ingredients of the filling together and fill the mixture inside each ball. Fry in hot ghee till golden brown.

Gravy

$1/2$ cups chopped onion	6 cloves garlic
3 tsps fresh ginger paste	250 gms tomatoes
1 cup curds	$1/4$ cup khoya
2 tsps ground spices	a few coriander leaves
$1 1/2$ tsps red chilli powder	3 tbsps ghee
4 green cardamoms	salt to taste

Fry the chopped onion and crushed cardamoms in ghee till brown. Add salt, garlic and ginger paste and one cup of water and stir till dry and onion is tender. Now add peeled and chopped tomatoes, curd, ground spices, red chilli powder and stir till gravy is thick. Pour 3 cups of water and cook again till gravy is a little thick. Then add koftas and mashed khoya. Cook till koftas are soft, sprinkle coriander leaves.

SAMBAR (SOUTH INDIAN)   serves 8

250 gms arhar dal	1 tsp turmeric
2 tbsps ghee	2 to 15 cups water
2 onions	60 gms tamarind
2 tsps mustard seed	3 medium tomatoes
200 gms drumsticks	4 whole red chillies
1 tsp methi seed	2 tsps white cuminseeds
15 gms kukum	salt to taste

Sambar powder: 4 tbsps coriander seeds, 12 black peppercorns, 6 whole red chillies and 1/2 fresh coconut.

Soak tamarind and kukum separately. Cook arhar dal with water, turmeric and 1 tbsp ghee until tender and no grain is seen. Cut drumsticks into 5 cm pieces and keep in hot water for 10 minutes. Remove from the water. Add to the dal drumsticks, sliced onions, big pieces of tomatoes and cook for ten minutes. Fry mustard seeds and four red chillies until brown, add methi seeds and fry until light brown, and add to dal. Now add tamarind pulp, kukum, salt and sambar powder and cook for ten minutes. If thick, add 2¹/₂ cups of hot water. Add chopped coriander leaves and ground white cuminseeds and cook for 5 minutes. Serve with dosa or rice.

SINDHI CURRY
serves 8

100 gms besan
$1/2$ cup ghee for frying besan
3 tsps turmeric
2 tsps methi seeds
1 tbsp white cuminseeds
5-6 dry mango pieces
60 gms tamarind
6 green chillies
120 gms drumsticks
150 gms cauliflower
150 gms potatoes
150 gms brinjal

30 gms kukum
10 cups water
a few mint leaves
2 tsps chopped coriander leaves
1 tsp ghee for frying fenugreek and cumin
1 tsp ghee for frying mustard
2 tsps mustard seeds
150 gms bhein or kamal kakri
60 gms peas

Soak kukum, tamarind and dry mango pieces separately. Fry besan in ghee until light brown, add water, turmeric, salt and big pieces of bhein. Fry methi and white cuminseeds until light brown and add to besan. Cook for 10 minutes. Add peas, brinjal, cauliflower and drumsticks, chopped green chillies, 4 whole chillies and potatoes and cook until tender. Put chopped coriander leaves, mint leaves, kukum, tamarind pulp, dry mango pieces and cook for a few minutes. Fry mustard in ghee and add to curry. Serve hot.

VEGETARIAN NARGASI KOFTA CURRY
serves 8

Kofta

$1/2$ kg bhein or kamal kakri
$1/2$ tsp yellow colour
$3/4$ cup roasted besan
2 tsps chopped ginger

200 gms paneer
2 tsps white cumin powder
2 green chillies
1 tsp chopped coriander leaves

36

salt to taste   ghee for deep frying

Boil bhein in salted water till tender. Strain, cool and
mash them. Mix cumin powder, roasted besan,
chopped green chilli, ginger, coriander and salt with
bhein. Take one-fourth of the paneer and mix with
yellow colour. Rub it till smooth. Make small round
balls and fill with mashed white paneer. Form into egg
shapes. Cover with bhein mixture and fry in deep ghee
till golden brown. Cool the koftas, cut into halves and
keep aside.

Curry

1 cup grated onion	4 cloves garlic
2 tsps chopped ginger	1 tsp red chilli powder
2 tsps white cumin powder	1 tsp ground spices
2 cloves	6 blanched almonds
4 green cardamoms	3 big tomatoes
$3/_4$ cup ghee	salt to taste

Fry the grated onion till golden brown, add ground
garlic and ginger and $1^1/_2$ cups water. Cook till dry.
Mix all the spices and peeled and chopped tomatoes,
red chilli powder and salt and stir till it leaves its ghee.
Add 4 cups of water and cook till $1^1/_2$ cups water is
left. Put the gravy in a dish, arrange koftas on it and
sprinkle coriander leaves.

BHUJIA

ARBI BHUJIA serves 8

1 kg arbi
$^1/_2$ tsp black pepper
$1^1/_2$ tsps turmeric
2 or 3 tbsps ghee
salt to taste

1 tsp red chilli powder
4 tsps amchoor
4 tsps white cumin powder
2 tsps chopped coriander
  leaves

Wash arbi and boil with $1^1/_2$ tsps salt in water. When tender, remove from the fire and peel. Press a little with hands and deep fry in ghee until brown. Heat 3 tbsps of ghee, add arbi, turmeric, salt, chilli powder, black pepper, coriander leaves, amchoor, white cumin powder and fry for 2 to 3 minutes. Remove from the fire and serve hot.

MASALA ARBI serves 8

1 kg arbi
3 tsps ground spices
120 gms onion
250 gms tomatoes
$^3/_4$ cup ghee
salt to taste

1 tsp turmeric
2 tsps coriander powder
2 tsps fresh ginger paste
2 tsps chopped coriander
  leaves

Peel, wash and dry the arbi. Cut into big pieces and fry until light brown. Heat the ghee and fry ground onion, ginger, turmeric and red chilli powder until light brown. Add arbi and fry it with masala until it is well browned. Then put peeled and chopped tomatoes in it and stir till a thick and smooth gravy is formed. Mix ground spices and coriander leaves with it.

ARBI WITH ONION *serves 8*

1 kg arbi
4 green chillies
360 gms onion
240 gms ghee

1 tsp turmeric
1 tsp black pepper
slices of 2 to 3 lemons
salt to taste

Scrape and wash the arbi and cut into round pieces.
Cut onion slices. Heat the ghee, fry onion, turmeric
and arbi on a low fire until golden brown and tender.
Add salt and black pepper. Serve hot with lemon
slices.

BRINJAL BHURTHA   *serves 4*

$^1/_2$ kg big brinjals
200 gms tomatoes
$^1/_2$ tsp red chilli powder
salt to taste

2 big onions
$^1/_2$ tsp black pepper
$^1/_2$ cup ghee

Roast whole brinjals over a charcoal fire or grill in an
oven placed on a wire rack. Turn them frequently until
tender and skin is burnt. Immerse in cold water and
peel the skin. Mash well. Heat ghee, fry chopped
onions until light brown and mix with mashed brinjals
and tomatoes (chopped). Stir until it leaves the sides
of pan. Remove from the fire, mix black pepper and
red chilli powder.

CAPSICUM BHUJIA   *serves 6*

250 gms capsicums
250 gms tomatoes
$^1/_2$ cup ghee
1 tsp chopped coriander
  leaves

125 gms onions
$^3/_4$ tsp turmeric
1 tsp ground spices
salt to taste

Cut onion into slices. Cut capsicums and tomatoes into big pieces. Heat the ghee, add turmeric, and fry capsicums, onions, and tomatoes together with salt until dry. Add ground spices and coriander leaves. Serve hot.

Variation: Potatoes can be added, if desired.

CAPSICUMS STUFFED WITH POTATOES
serves 6

250 gms capsicums	350 gms boiled potatoes
2 to 3 green chillies	1 tsp chopped coriander
2 tsps chopped fresh	leaves
ginger	$1/2$ cup ghee
$1/2$ tsp turmeric	$1/2$ tsp ground spices
1 tbsp amchoor	salt to taste

Chop the boiled potatoes and green chillies. Heat ghee, add turmeric and fry the chopped ingredients for a few minutes. Remove from the fire, add salt, ground spices and amchoor and mix well. Slit the capsicums lengthwise, fill the cooked potatoes inside. Put them in the same pan and cover. Cook on a very low fire until tender.

CAPSICUMS STUFFED WITH SPICES
serves 4

250 gms capsicums	$1/2$ tsp turmeric
3 tsps white cumin powder	3 tsps coriander powder
2 ground cloves	1 tbsp amchoor
$1/2$ tsp black pepper	$1/4$ tsp cinnamon powder
$1/2$ kg curds	$1/2$ cup ghee
$1/4$ tsp asafoetida	salt to taste

Heat ghee, put asafoetida, then add turmeric, curds, ground spices, salt and pepper and stir until browned. Remove from the fire, add amchoor and cool. Silt the capsicums lengthwise and fill the fried spices in them. Cover the pan and cook on a low heat until capsicums are tender.

FRIED CHANA WITH GRAVY   *serves 8*

$^1/_2$ kg kabuli chana
2 level tsps soda
  bicarbonate
1 tbsp ghee
4 tsps ground spices
2 tsps white cumin
  powder
1 tsp chilli powder for
  tamarind
60 gms ginger slices

6 cups water
$1^1/_2$ tsps red chilli powder
4 tsps salt for the masala
  below
8 tsps amchoor
120 gms tamarind
250 gms tomatoes
4 medium onions
8 green chillies

Soak the chana overnight in water with soda bicarbonate. Heat ghee, put red chilli powder and soaked chana and boil in the same water until tender. Add salt, amchoor, spices and cuminseed powder and mix it lightly. Cut onions into slices and tomatoes into medium pieces. Cut ginger into long strips. Soak tamarind in $1^1/_2$ cups of water, pass through a sieve and mix with red chilli powder. Serve onion, tomatoes, green chillies and tamarind pulp separately. Serve hot with plain puree.

KHATTA CHANA   *serves 10*

$^1/_2$ kg chana
1 tsp salt
8 cups water

1 tsp tea leaves
2 tsps soda bicarbonate

Soak chana with tea leaves tied in a muslin cloth and soda bicarbonate overnight in water. Boil with salt till quite tender on a low fire. Put it in a strainer to drain water. Then mix the following ingredients in the boiled chana:

4 sliced lemons	4 tsps salt
12 green chillies	120 gms onion slices
250 gms tomatoes	60 gms ginger
4 tsp chopped coriander leaves	2 tsps turmeric
	4 tsps black pepper
60 gms pomegranate seeds	2 tsps black cumin powder
	1 tsp amchoor
1 tsp red chilli powder	1 cup melted ghee

Cut ginger into long strips. Grind pomegranate seeds finely with one cup of water and strain. Put in a pan. Mix salt, turmeric, ground spices and pepper with chana and cook in pomegranate water for a few minutes. Pour smoking hot ghee over them. Sprinkle with ginger, coriander, halved green chillies, onion, lemon and tomato slices.

SPECIAL SOOKHA CHANA   serves 10

$^1/_2$ kg kabuli chana	2 cm piece cinnamon
4 cloves	2 tsps soda bicarbonate
6 cardamoms	1 medium piece ginger
$7^1/_2$ cups water	2 tsps salt

Wash and soak the chana in water with all the ingredients, except salt, overnight. Boil with salt on low fire until quite tender. Put in a strainer and remove all the spices.

Masala

5 tsps ginger	4 tsps chopped green
200 gms boiled potatoes	coriander leaves

10 green chillies
1 cup butter or ghee
3 tsps black pepper
2 tsps coriander powder
4 tsps black cumin
  powder
$^1/_2$ tsp cinnamon powder
3 to 4 tsps amchoor
4 to 5 tsps salt

3 lemons
250 gms tomatoes
$^1/_4$ tsp grated nutmeg
$^1/_2$ tsp ground cloves
3 tsps white cumin powder
$^1/_2$ tsp ground big
  cardamoms
5 gms black salt

Mix lightly three-fourths of the ground ingredients, small pieces of potatoes, long slices of ginger and chopped coriander leaves in chana. Heat the ghee and pour over chana, then add 1 cup of boiling water and mix well. Put the vessel on very low fire for 10 minutes. Sprinkle the rest of the ground spices before serving. Decorate with green chillies and tomato pieces.

LADYSFINGER BHUJIA—I   serves 6

$^1/_2$ kg ladysfinger
$^1/_2$ cup ghee
$^3/_4$ tsp turmeric

250 gms onions
1 tsp black pepper
salt to taste

Cut the onion into slices and ladysfingers into small pieces. Heat the ghee, add turmeric and fry ladysfingers for 5 minutes and add onions, salt and pepper and stir on a low fire until the onions and ladysfingers are tender and light brown in colour. Serve hot.

LADYSFINGER BHUJIA—II   serves 6

$^1/_2$ kg ladysfingers
1 tsp black pepper

1 tsp turmeric
2 tsps amchoor

2 tsps ground spices $^1/_2$ cup ghee
250 gms onions, sliced   salt to taste

Fry the onion until light brown. Remove from the ghee and fry ladysfingers cut in small pieces, until light brown. Mix turmeric, salt, pepper, amchoor, fried onions and ground spices with fried ladysfingers and stir for a few minutes.

LADYSFINGERS IN CURD   *serves 6*

$^1/_2$ kg ladysfingers $^1/_2$ cup ghee
$1^1/_2$ tbsp coriander powder   1 tsp turmeric
$^1/_2$ tsp red chilli powder $^1/_2$ cup curds
1 tsp ground spices   salt to taste

Wash and dry ladysfingers. Cut from both ends. Heat the ghee and fry them whole until golden brown. Remove, fry coriander, cuminseeds, turmeric and red chilli powder until light brown. Add beaten curds and salt and stir for a few minutes until thick. Mix fried ladysfingers and ground spices with the thick gravy and stir for a few minutes. Serve hot.

LADYSFINGERS IN
TOMATO SAUCE   *serves 6*

$^1/_2$ kg ladysfingers $^1/_2$ kg tomatoes
1 tsp chopped ginger   1 spring onion
$^1/_4$ tsp red chilli powder   2 cloves
6 peppercorns $^1/_2$ cup ghee
salt to taste

Wash and dry the ladysfingers. Fry them whole with a little salt in ghee until light brown and tender. Remove. Chop spring onion and tomatoes. Cook the chopped ingredients, salt, cloves, peppercorns and red chilli powder together in a pan until tender. Pass through a sieve. Heat it and then mix with fried ladysfingers and stir for a few minutes.

STUFFED LADYSFINGERS   *serves 5*

$^1/_2$ kg ladysfingers
1 tsp turmeric
1 tsp black pepper
1 tsp salt

1 tbsp amchoor
1 tsp coriander powder
$^1/_2$ cup ghee

Wash the ladysfingers and dry with a cloth, remove both ends and slit lengthwise. Mix amchoor, turmeric, salt, coriander and black pepper together and stuff in ladysfingers. Heat ghee, fry them on a low fire until light brown and tender. Serve hot.

MAKHANI TOMATO PANEER   *serves 6*

$^1/_2$ kg tomato
$^1/_4$ cup butter
$^1/_2$ tsp red chilli powder
250 gms paneer
salt to taste

2 cloves
3 tsps sugar
a few coriander leaves
1 tsp fresh ginger paste

Cook chopped tomatoes and cloves till tender. Pass through a sieve. Mix sugar, salt, red chilli powder, ground ginger with tomato pulp. Cook for 5 minutes, add thick pieces of paneer, coriander leaves and continue cooking till a little thick. Add butter. Serve hot.

METHI PANEER   *serves 6*

250 gms methi
500 gms paneer

1 cup ghee
$^1/_2$ tsp red chilli powder

$^1/_4$ black pepper $^1/_2$ tsp turmeric
1 tsp ground spices   1 tsp coriander powder
$^1/_2$ tsp cumin powder   salt to taste

Cut the paneer into small cubes and fry in ghee till golden brown. Keep aside. Clean and wash methi leaves. Boil in salted water, drain and grind finely. Heat the ghee, fry ground methi with turmeric until it leaves the ghee, add fried paneer, red chilli powder, salt, ground spices, black pepper, coriander, white cuminseeds and two cups of water and cook on a low fire till tender and almost dry.

POTATO BHUJIA   *serves 6*

$^1/_2$ kg potatoes   120 gms ghee
1 tbsp amchoor   2 tsps chopped coriander
1 tsp chopped green chilli   leaves
$^1/_2$ tsp black pepper   1 tsp white cuminseeds
salt to taste

Boil potatoes in salted water until tender. Peel and cut into small pieces. Heat the ghee, fry cuminseeds and then add potatoes, chopped coriander, green chilli, salt, pepper, and amchoor and stir for a few minutes until well mixed.

DAHIWALE ALOO   *serves 6*

$^1/_2$ kg medium potatoes   250 gms curd
1 tsp white cumin powder   1 tsp turmeric
1 tsp chopped coriander   1 tsp chopped green
   leaves   chillies
2 tsps ground spices $^1/_2$ tsp red chilli powder
$^1/_2$ cup ghee   salt to taste

Deep fry peeled whole potatoes in ghee on a low fire

until light brown. Remove from the ghee. Now heat $1/_2$ cup ghee, add cuminseed powder, turmeric, red chilli powder and curds and stir until light brown. Add fried potatoes, salt and $1^1/_2$ to 2 cups of water and cook on a low fire until potatoes are tender. Mix chopped coriander, green chillies and spices. Remove from the fire and serve.

DUM ALOO   *serves 8*

$3/_4$ kg medium potatoes $1/_2$ cup ghee
1 tsp Kashmiri mirch $1/_2$ tsp asafoetida water
$1^1/_2$ tsp white cumin   1 cup curds
   powder $1/_2$ tsp fresh ginger paste
1 tsp ground spices   salt to taste
a few coriander leaves

Boil the potatoes in salt water. Peel and prick them with a toothpick. Deep fry in ghee on a low fire until brown. Melt the ghee in a vessel and add the curds, ground cuminseeds and asafoetida and cook. When the curd becomes golden brown, add a little water and cook till the gravy is slightly thick, then add the potatoes. Sprinkle with coriander leaves and ground spices and cover the vessel and simmer for a few minutes. Serve hot.

STUFFED POTATO BHUJIA   *serves 10*

1 kg potatoes   3 tbsps tomato sauce
$1/_2$ cup ghee   2 tsps red chilli powder
3 tsps cumin powder   3 tsps ground spices
2 tsps fresh ginger paste   3 tsps chopped coriander
$1/_2$ tsp turmeric   leaves
5 gms almonds   5 gms raisins
$1/_4$ tsp asafoetida water   4 cups khoya
salt to taste   2 cups curds

Boil the potatoes in salt water until nearly tender. Peel and scoop out the potatoes. Fry tomato sauce, chopped ginger, raisins, almonds and khoya for a few minutes. Fill in potatoes and close the top with mashed potatoes. Secure each with toothpicks and deep fry in ghee until brown.

Gravy

Melt the ghee, add asafoetida water, cover and cook for two minutes. Add the beaten curds and fry for a few minutes until it becomes light brown. Add turmeric, red chilli and cumin powder, salt and $1^1/_2$ cups of water. Cook till boiling point and then add fried potatoes, chopped coriander leaves and spices. Cover the vessel. Cook on very low fire for a few minutes.

SPECIAL POTATO BHUJIA serves 6

$^1/_2$ kg potatoes	1 tomato
1 tsp long strips of ginger	2 green chillies
few coriander leaves	1 tsp methi leaves
2 tsps black pepper	1 tsp cumin powder
4 tsps ground spices	$^1/_2$ tsp black salt
4 tsps ground	$^1/_4$ tsp grated nutmeg
pomegranate seeds	$^1/_2$ cup melted ghee
2 tsps salt	250 gms peas

Boil the potatoes with $^1/_2$ tsp salt till they become tender. Peel and cut into long pieces, and mix with all the ground ingredients. Cut the tomatoes into quarters, remove the pulp from them and then cut into very small pieces. Boil the peas with $^1/_8$ tsp soda bicarbonate. Now mix boiled peas, thin long strips of ginger, chopped green chillies, coriander leaves and small pieces of tomatoes with potatoes. Finally, pour smoking hot ghee over the potatoes at the time of serving.

STUFFED POTATO CHOPS
WITH TOMATO SAUCE   *serves 6*

$^1/_2$ kg potatoes
250 gms peas
2 carrots
1 tsp chopped fresh
   ginger
3 tsps tomato ketchup
ghee for deep frying
1 tsp ground spices
$^1/_2$ tsp turmeric

250 gms cauliflower
2 tsps chopped coriander
   leaves
3 green chillies
2 tsps chopped onion
breadcrumbs for coating
$^1/_2$ cup flour for batter
$^1/_2$ tsp black pepper
salt to taste

Boil the potatoes in salt water till tender. Cool and grate them. Boil finely chopped carrots in salt water till tender. Fry chopped onion and ginger in one tbsp of ghee for one minute. Add turmeric, chopped cauliflower, peas, salt, coriander leaves, green chillies, black pepper and ground spices and fry for two minutes. Now add water and cook till the vegetables are tender and dry. Then mix tomato ketchup and cool. Mix boiled carrot and a little salt with the grated potatoes. Fill cooked cauliflower in small portions of the grated potato and carrot mixture and shape into chops. Dust with flour, dip into flour batter and roll in breadcrumbs. Fry in hot ghee till golden brown. Drain, and serve in an oval plate. Decorate all round with fried potato chips.

SPINACH AND
CHANA DAL BHUJIA   *serves 6*

1 kg spinach
1 big tomato
$^3/_4$ tsp red chilli powder
salt to taste

60 gms chana dal
2 tsps chopped ginger
$^1/_2$ cup ghee

Pick and wash chana dal and soak in water for 15 minutes. Wash and chop the spinach. Cook spinach and dal together until tender. Fry ginger in ghee with salt, red chilli powder and chopped tomato; add chana dal and spinach and cook until dry. Serve hot at lunch or dinner.

SPINACH AND MOONG DAL BHUJIA serves 6

In the recipe above substitute moong dal for chana dal.

PANEER AND SPINACH BHUJIA serves 6

750 gms spinach
$^1/_2$ cup curds
100 gms blanched
   tomatoes
200 gms paneer
6 cloves garlic
2 onions

75 gms khoya
1 tsp soda bicarbonate
$^3/_4$ cup ghee
1 tsp fresh ginger paste
1 tsp chilli powder
2 tsps ground spices
salt to taste

Cut paneer into small pieces and fry until golden brown. Cook spinach with 1 tsp of soda bicarbonate until tender. Grind it finely. Fry chopped onion and garlic until brown, add a little water and cook until onion is soft. Now add ground ginger, chopped tomatoes, salt, red chilli powder and cook until a thick gravy is formed. Add spinach and curd and fry for a few minutes. Add fried paneer and stir until spinach leaves the ghee, then add mashed khoya and ground spices and cook for a few minutes. Serve hot.

SPINACH AND POTATO BHUJIA   *serves 6*

1 kg spinach	350 gms potatoes
$^1/_2$ cup ghee	$^1/_2$ cup curds
1 tsp red chilli powder	$^1/_2$ tsp turmeric
1 tsp ground spices	salt to taste

Peel and cut poatoes into small pieces and deep fry in ghee until light brown. Wash and chop spinach. Heat the ghee, add turmeric, spinach, red chilli powder and salt and cook on medium fire until dry. Add fried potatoes and curds. Stir and cook on low fire until it leaves the sides of the pan. Mix with ground spices. Serve hot.

SPINACH AND ONION BHUJIA   *serves 6*

1 kg spinach	$^1/_2$ cup ghee
2 tsps ginger paste	$^1/_2$ tsp garlic paste
250 gms onion	2 tsps ground spices
120 gms tomatoes	$^1/_2$ tsp turmeric
1 tsp red chilli powder	salt to taste

Cut onion into thin slices. Chop washed spinach. Heat ghee, fry garlic until light brown; add onion slices, spinach ginger, salt, turmeric, red chilli powder, chopped tomatoes and cook on a low fire until dry. Now stir until it leaves the sides of the pan clear. Remove from the fire.

STUFFED TOMATOES   *serves 10*

750 gms tomatoes	200 gms french beans
3 carrots	1 turnip
200 gms peas	250 gms potatoes
$1^1/_2$ onions	2 tsps fresh ginger pieces
3 to 4 green chillies	4 tsps flour
a few coriander leaves	$^3/_4$ tsp black pepper

| 1½ tbsps ghee | 8 tsps tomato ketchup |
| 2 tsps cumin powder | salt to taste |

Scoop out the pulp from tomatoes. Steam all chopped vegetables and boil potatoes. Fry chopped onion, ginger and green chillies until light brown; then add salt, black pepper and flour and fry. Add two tbsps of tomato pulp, steamed vegetables and small pieces of potatoes and cook for five minutes until dry. Cool and fill the mixture in tomatoes. Heat the ghee in a frying pan, put stuffed tomatoes, cuminseeds and tomato ketchup in it. Add ½ tsp salt and cook for 3 minutes. Turn the tomatoes and again cook for 2 minutes. Remove from the fire. Serve hot with potato chips.

Potato chips

Peel and cut 250 gms potatoes thinly. Soak in water for half an hour. Deep fry in ghee until light brown. Remove and drain off oil. Sprinkle with salt and serve hot.

TINDA BHUJIA *serves 6*

½ kg tinda	2 big onions
3 tsps fresh ginger paste	9 garlic cloves
2 tsps coriander leaves	1 tsp white cuminseeds
2 tsps ground spices	½ teacup curds
9 green cardamoms	2 tomatoes
1 tsp red chilli powder	60 gms khoya
2 tbsps ghee	salt to taste

Peel the tinda and make four cuts in each. Deep fry in ghee until light brown. Fry ground onion, garlic and green cardamoms until brown; add one cup of water, red chilli powder, ginger and stir until onion is tender. Now add ground spices, ground coriander and coarsely ground white cuminseeds, curds, chopped tomatoes and fried tinda and stir until gravy is cooked. Add khoya and stir for 2 minutes.

DALS

MOONG DAL
serves 6

250 gms dal
1 tsp salt
1 small onion
$^1/_4$ tsp red chilli powder
$4^1/_2$ cups water

$^1/_2$ tsp turmeric
$^1/_2$ tsp black cuminseeds
1 tsp ginger slices
$^1/_4$ cup ghee

Pick and wash the dal and put in a vessel with turmeric, salt and water. Cook till tender. Heat the ghee, fry whole black cuminseeds, chopped onion and ginger, according to taste, then mix with dal. Serve hot. (Arhar, Moth, Masoor, Chana, Urad and Moong dal without husk can be cooked similarly.)

FRIED URAD DAL
serves 6

2 cups urad dal
2 tsps turmeric
1 tsp black cuminseeds
2 tsps ginger
1 big onion
2 green chillies
salt to taste

5 cups water
1 tsp black pepper
2 medium tomatoes
$^1/_2$ to $^3/_4$ cup butter or
   ghee
2 tsps chopped coriander
   leaves

Wash and soak the dal for 15 minutes. Fry chopped onion and ginger in butter/ghee until light brown, add cuminseeds and fry for 1 minute. Now add chopped tomatoes and stir for a while and keep aside. Boil water, add dal, turmeric and salt and cook on a low fire. When dal is nearly cooked, add the above mixture and chopped tomatoes, coriander, green chillies and black pepper and cook for 5 minutes.

MUGLAI DAL   *serves 6*

$1^1/_2$ cups urad dal $3^1/_2$ cups water
  (without husk)   120 gms paneer
1 tsp turmeric   4 green chillies
1 tsp black pepper $^3/_4$ tsp black cuminseeds
few coriander leaves   1 small onion
2 tsps chopped ginger $^1/_4$ cup ghee
1 medium firm tomato $^1/_4$ cup cream
salt to taste

Soak urad dal for one hour. Boil water with turmeric and salt. Add the dal and cook till it becomes tender and each grain is separate. Put it in a strainer to remove excess water. Heat the ghee, fry finely chopped onion and ginger till onion is golden brown. Then add black cuminseeds and fry for a second and mix with the dal; also add finely chopped green chillies and coriander leaves. Put fried pieces of paneer in it.

At the time of serving, put the dal in a dish and garnish with chopped tomato without pulp and then pour cream over it.

PANCHRATNI DAL   *serves 6*

60 gms chana dal   60 gms whole moong dal
60 gms whole urad dal   60 gms whole masoor dal
30 gms arhar dal   1 tsp turmeric
2 tsps fresh ginger paste   a tiny piece of asafoetida
$^1/_3$ cup ghee $^1/_2$ tsp red chilli powder
$^1/_2$ tsp black pepper   1 tsp black cuminseeds

1 big tomato   1 small onion
2 green chillies, chopped   1 tbsp curds
salt to taste

Pick and wash the dals. Boil enough water and add
the dals and turmeric and cook them until half tender.
Heat 1 tbsp ghee and fry asafoetida until light brown
and crush it. Mix it with half-cooked dals with some
ghee, salt and curds and cook until tender and well
mixed. Mix red chilli powder and black pepper. Heat
ghee, fry chopped onion and ginger until light brown,
add black cuminseeds, chopped green chillies and
tomatoes without pulp and stir for a few minutes. Mix
with the dal.

RASAM (SOUTH INDIAN)   *serves 6*

120 gms arhar dal   60 gms tamarind
5 cups water   1 tsp red chilli powder
4 drops of asafoetida   3 tsps mustard seeds
    water   2 tbsps ghee
2 tomatoes   2 tbsps jaggery
4 green chillies   4 whole red chillies
3 tsps coriander   10 black peppercorns
60 gms fresh coconut   salt to taste

Pick and wash the dal and cook with water until
tender. Pass through a sieve. Soak tamarind in a cup
of water for 10 minutes, and pass through a sieve.
Grind coriander, red chillies, coconut and black
pepper finely with a little water. Put all the ingredients
into mashed dal, its water, ghee, and coriander leaves
and cook until a little thick. Remove from the fire. Fry
mustard seeds in ghee and mix with rasam. Sprinkle
with chopped coriander leaves. Serve hot with boiled
rice.

SHAHI DAL
serves 6

250 gms urad dal
1 cup water
1 tomato without pulp
$^1/_4$ tsp black pepper
$^1/_2$ tsp red chilli powder
1 tsp chopped ginger
1 small onion
$^1/_2$ cup ghee
salt to taste

$2^1/_2$ cups milk
4 green cardamoms
8 blanched almonds,
  slit into halves
$^1/_2$ tsp turmeric
2 tsps chopped coriander
  leaves
$^1/_2$ tsp black cuminseeds

Pick and wash the dal. Put dal, milk, water, $^1/_4$ cup ghee, turmeric, red chilli powder, cardamoms, salt and almonds and cook on a low fire until tender and water and milk are evaporated and each grain is separated. Heat the remaining ghee, fry chopped onion and ginger until light brown. Then add black cuminseeds, chopped tomato and coriander leaves and stir for one minute. Mix with cooked dal and sprinkle black pepper.

SPECIAL MIXED DAL
serves 6

60 gms moong dal
  without husk
60 gms chana dal
15 cups water
1 tsp turmeric
$^1/_2$ cup ghee
2 tsps chopped fresh
  ginger
1 tsp black cuminseeds
$^1/_2$ tsp black pepper
1 bay leaf

60 gms urad dal without
  husk
60 gms whole masoor dal
2 tsps ground spices
a tiny piece of asafoetida
1 big onion
1 tsp white cuminseeds
$^1/_2$ tsp red chilli powder
salt to taste
120 gms curds
2 whole red chillies

Pick, wash and soak all the dals overnight. Remove their husk. Boil water, add the dals, white cuminseeds, salt, asafoetida and ginger and cook until tender. Add the curds, red chilli powder and black pepper and cook until well mixed. Heat the ghee, fry bay leaf, whole red chillies and chopped onion until light brown; add black cuminseeds and stir for a minute. Mix with the dal and cook for a few minutes. Sprinkle ground spices. Serve hot with chapatis or boiled rice.

URAD AND CHANA DAL   serves 6

120 gms urad dal
   without husk
4 cups water
$^1/_2$ tsp red chilli powder
1 tsp black cuminseeds
1 tsp chopped ginger
salt to taste

120 gms chana dal
   without husk
1 tsp turmeric
$^1/_2$ tsp black pepper
1 small onion
$^1/_2$ cup ghee

Pick, wash and soak the dals for 25 minutes. Boil water, add the dals, turmeric, salt, red chilli powder and cook on low fire until tender and well mixed. Heat the ghee, fry chopped onion and ginger until light brown; add cuminseeds and pepper and stir for a minute. Pour over the dal and serve.

SABUT URAD DAL   serves 12

$^1/_2$ kg sabut urad dal
1 tsp black pepper
6 cloves garlic
1 tsp black cuminseeds
2 tsps chopped ginger
salt to taste

15 cups water
a few drops of asafoetida
   water
1 onion
2 tbsps ghee

Pick and wash the urad dal. Boil water, add urad dal and cook on low fire until half tender. Add asafoetida water, black pepper, chopped garlic, ginger and onion and cook until tender and well mixed. Heat the ghee, fry black cuminseeds till they splutter and mix with the dal.

RAITA

BRINJAL RAITA   *serves 6*

1 big brinjal (350 gms) $^1/_2$ kg curds
1 tsp chopped mint leaves $^1/_2$ tsp black cuminseeds
$^1/_2$ tsp black pepper $^1/_2$ tsp red chilli powder
salt to taste

Grill the whole brinjal over charcoal fire or bake in an oven on a wire rack until tender and the skin is burnt. Put in cold water, remove the skin, and mash it. Beat the curds with salt, red chilli powder, black pepper and cuminseeds and then mix the mashed brinjal and mint leaves. Serve cold. (If raita is thick, add 3 to 4 tbsps water and mix well.)

DAHI BARA   *serves 10*

350 gms urad dal   1 tsp black pepper
$^1/_4$ tsp red chilli powder   1 tsp chopped coriander
2 chopped green chillies   leaves
$^1/_2$ tsp black cuminseeds   1 tsp ground spices
ghee for deep frying $^1/_4$ tsp soda bicarbonate
salt to taste   1 kg curds

Soak urad dal overnight, then remove the husk by repeatedly washing it with water. Grind it finely and mix green chillies, coriander, ground spices, chilli powder and soda bicarbonate and beat it until light. Wet the palm of the hand with a little water, put a little dal mixture and form into round and flat balls. Gently drop the balls one by one into hot ghee. Fry until evenly browned on both sides. Drain well, and immerse in cold water. Beat the curds with salt, black pepper, red chilli powder and black cuminseeds. If the curd is too thick, add a few tbsps of water. Squeeze out the water carefully from the 'bara' (press them between the palms of the hands without breaking) and drop them in curds. Garnish with mint leaves and red chilli powder. Serve cold.

KHEERA RAITA   serves 10

250 gms cucumber $^1/_2$ kg curds
$^1/_2$ tsp black cuminseeds   1 tsp black pepper
1 tbsp water   1 tsp chopped mint leaves
salt to taste

Peel the cucumber and grate it. Boil the water, put grated cucumber and cook for two minutes until half tender. Remove from the fire, cool and squeeze out the water. Beat the curds and mix cucumber, salt, black pepper, mint leaves and cuminseeds. Serve cold.

MINT RAITA   serves 6

$^1/_2$ kg curds   1 tbsp ground mint leaves
1 green chilli, ground $^1/_2$ tsp black pepper
salt to taste

Beat the curds and mix with green chilli, mint leaves, salt and black pepper. Serve cold.

ONION RAITA   serves 6

$^1/_2$ kg curds   120 gms onions, sliced
2 green chillies   1 tsp chopped mint leaves
1 tsp black cuminseeds $^1/_2$ tsp black pepper
$^1/_2$ tsp red chilli powder   salt to taste

60

Rub 1 tsp salt with onion slices, keep aside for 10 minutes and wash them. Beat the curd with salt, pepper, red chilli powder, cuminseeds and chopped green chillies and mix with onion slices and chopped mint leaves. Serve cold.

PAKORI RAITA   serves 6

$^1/_2$ kg curds $^1/_2$ tsp black cuminseeds
1 tsp chopped mint leaves $^1/_2$ tsp black pepper
$^1/_2$ tsp red chilli powder   150 gms besan
ghee for frying   salt to taste

Make batter of besan with water to a thick dropping consistency. Heat the ghee in a deep pan, pour the batter through a big-holed skimmer, pressing with hand lightly over so that the drops fall into the ghee. Fry for 2 minutes and then turn over. When they become crisp remove from the ghee and drop into cold water. Beat the curds with salt, pepper, red chilli powder and black cuminseeds. Squeeze out the water carefully from the pakoris (press them between the palms of the hands without breaking). Put in curds and decorate with $^1/_4$ tsp red chilli powder and mint leaves. Serve cold.

LAUKI RAITA   serves 6

250 gms lauki $^1/_2$ kg curds
2 green chillies $^1/_2$ tsp black pepper
$^1/_4$ tsp red chilli powder $^1/_2$ tsp black cuminseeds
2 tsps chopped mint leaves salt to taste

Peel and grate the lauki, boil in water until tender. Remove from the fire. Drain and cool. Beat the curd, mix with salt, pepper, cuminseeds, chopped green chillies, mint leaves, and the lauki. Serve cold.

POTATO RAITA   *serves 6*

See the recipe of lauki raita. Use the same ingredients and method except add boiled and cubed potatoes instead of lauki. Tomato raita can be made in the same way.

SWEET RAITA   *serves 6*

$^1/_2$ kg curds   150 gms raisins
$^1/_2$ tsp black pepper   120 gms sugar
1 tsp salt

Clean the raisins and soak them in water for two hours. Beat the curds with sugar, salt and pepper and put soaked raisins in it.

SNACKS

MIXED VEGETABLE PAKORAS   *serves 8*

2 cups besan
$1/_2$ tsp red chilli powder
4 small pieces of
    cauliflower
1 big potato
a few spinach leaves
1 to $1^1/_2$ cups water

$1/_8$ tsp baking powder
1 tsp chopped coriander
    leaves
1 small brinjal
1 medium onion
ghee for deep frying
salt to taste

Peel and cut vegetables into small and thin pieces. Make a thick batter with besan, water, salt, baking powder and coriander leaves. Sprinkle red chilli powder and a little salt on the vegetables and then dip them in the batter. Fry in hot ghee till golden brown and crisp. Serve immediately.

MANGO PAKORAS   *serves 8*

2 mangoes, half ripe
1 big onion
$1/_2$ tsp red chilli powder
3 green chillies
4 pieces ginger
$1^1/_2$ cups water
salt to taste

$1/_2$ tsp ground spices
1 tsp white cuminseeds
a few mint and green
    coriander leaves
$1/_8$ tsp thymol seeds
2 cups besan
ghee or oil for deep frying

Mix besan and salt and make a batter by adding water. Whisk the mixture; test its lightness by putting a drop of the batter in water. If it floats, it is ready. Chop the onion, ginger, green chilli, mint and

63

coriander leaves. Peel the mangoes and chop into small flat pieces. Add all the chopped ingredients into the mixture and mix it. Deep fry spoonsful of the mixture in ghee. Turn over and remove with a perforated flat spoon or jharna when browned. Serve hot.

PANEER PAKORAS serves 8

$1^1/_2$ cups besan   250 gms paneer
$^1/_8$ tsp baking powder $^1/_4$ tsp thymol seeds
$^1/_2$ tsp red chilli powder   salt to taste
ghee for deep frying

Make a thick batter of besan with water, salt, ground thymol seeds, red chilli powder and baking powder. Cut paneer into big thin pieces and rub with a little salt. Dip the pieces in the batter. Fry in hot ghee till golden brown and crisp. Serve immediately.

POTATO BONDAS
(SOUTH INDIAN) serves 8

$^1/_2$ kg potatoes $^3/_4$ cup onion
3 green chillies   1 tsp chopped coriander
1 tsp chopped fresh ginger   leaves
$^1/_4$ tsp mustard seeds $^1/_4$ tsp turmeric
2 cups besan   3 tsps ghee
$1^1/_2$ cups water   mustard oil for deep frying
salt to taste

Boil the potatoes. Cool, peel and chop them. Chop onion, and green chillies. Heat the ghee, add turmeric and fry onion, ginger, green chillies with salt and mustard seeds for one minute. Add potatoes and stir for a few minutes. Remove from the fire. Mix green coriander and cool. Take sufficient potato mixture to form a ball the size of a billiard ball. Make a batter of thick dropping consistency with besan and water, add salt. Dip potato balls in it and fry in very hot oil until golden brown. Serve hot.

CLUB SANDWICHES   *serves 8*

12 slices of bread	butter
1 level tsp	$1/4$ tsp white pepper
mustard powder	$1/2$ tsp salt
3 gherkins	6 pickled onions
$3/4$ cup cashewnuts	250 gms potatoes
3 tomatoes	1 tbsp cream
2 cucumbers	cheese slices

Cream the butter. Add cream, mustard powder, chopped gherkins and pickled onions and mix well. Brown the bread slices on one side and spread butter mixture on the unbrowned side of slices. On it put cheese slices, tomato slices, cucumber and then again the buttered side of the slice. Press well together. Fasten with 4 toothpicks and cut into 4 triangles. Put them on a plate and decorate with fried cashewnuts and potato wafers. Serve at tea. (Fry cashewnuts in hot ghee till light brown. Drain on paper and sprinkle salt over them.)

RUSSIAN SANDWICHES   *serves 12*

8 tsps butter	1 tin cream cheese
1 tsp red chilli sauce	(400 gms)
1 or $1^1/2$ tsp tomato	$1/2$ tsp salt
ketchup	$1/2$ tsp mustard powder
$1/2$ cup cheese	1 kg bread

Mix butter, tomato ketchup, salt, chilli sauce and mustard powder to a soft paste. Grate the cheese. Cut

65

bread lengthwise in $^1/_2$ cm thick slices. Remove the hard crusts. Spread the soft paste with a flat knife and then grated cheese. Roll up and wrap each roll in butter paper and fix it with toothpicks and chill. Before serving, cut into $^1/_2$ cm thick slices. Serve with tea.

FRUIT GAZAK   *serves 6*

15 gms almonds	15 gms cashewnuts
15 gms peanuts	15 gms walnuts
200 gms sugar	15 gms butter
6 green cardamoms	1 tsp kewra flavour

Mix all the dry nuts and brown to a gold colour in a moderate oven to remove the raw flavour. Melt sugar on very low fire, add crushed nuts, butter, crushed cardamoms and kewra and stir. Remove from the fire. Pour on a greased wooden board and roll out quickly with a rolling pin into 1 cm thickness. Cut immediately into long strips, about $2^1/_2$ cms long, and store in an airtight jar.

DELHI MATHI   *serves 8*

250 gms flour	$3^1/_2$ tsps melted ghee
1 level tsp salt	$^1/_2$ tsp caraway seed
6 tbsps water	ghee for deep frying

Sift the flour and put all the ingredients together in a bowl. Rub with fingertips and then knead with water. Make 18 to 20 round balls. Roll into very thin rounds. Fold into a triangle-shaped mathi. Press the pointed side with the rolling pin (but be careful not to press the layers). Deep fry in ghee on medium fire. Turn it frequently until brown. Drain on a wire rack. Serve at tea.

PUNJABI MATHI *serves 8*

250 gms flour
$^1/_2$ tsp ajwain seeds
60 gms ghee
$^1/_4$ cup water
1 tsp salt

1 tsp peppercorn
2 tsps curds
$^1/_4$ tsp soda bicarbonate
ghee for deep frying

Sift the flour. Put ajwain, curds, salt, ghee, water, and soda in the centre of the flour and mix well into a soft dough. Add peppercorns. Make 30 round balls, then press each with a rolling pin. Heat ghee, remove from the fire, put mathis in it, leave for 5 minutes and then put on fire again and fry until light brown. Remove the karahi from the fire, turn the mathis and leave in ghee for a few minutes. Again put the karahi on fire and fry until brown and turn frequently. Drain on a strainer or a wire rack.

PUNJABI KACHORI *serves 8*

Dough

250 gms flour
$^1/_2$ tsp salt
$^3/_4$ to 1 cup lukewarm water

60 gms ghee for the flour
3 tsps curds
ghee for deep frying

Sift the flour, mix with ghee, salt, water and curds and knead until smooth. Make 16 round balls. Press each in the centre, place a little of the filling and close it. First press the sides with the palm of the hand and then press a little from the centre. Heat the ghee (not very hot), then remove from the fire. Put a kachori in it and leave it for two minutes. Press with a skimmer until it comes up. Now fry it on medium fire until light brown.

Filling

2 tsps suji	$1/4$ tsp soda bicarbonate
$1/4$ tsp salt	$1/4$ tsp red chilli powder
120 gms split urad dal	$1^1/2$ tsps black
2 tsps ground coriander	cuminseeds

Soak the urad dal overnight. Remove the husk by rubbing and washing it repeatedly with water. Grind it finely, add salt, spices and soda bicarbonate. Beat to a soft and smooth mixture, then add semolina and mix well.

VEGETABLE SAMOSA   serves 12

Covering

$1/2$ kg flour	8 tbsps melted ghee
1 level tsp salt	8 tbsps water

Sift the flour and salt and add ghee. Rub with fingertips, then knead it with water. Make 2 dozen balls. Roll out each into a thin round and then cut into half. Wet the edges of one half and make a cone with it. Fill cooked potatoes in it and press the edges together. Put in ghee and deep fry until light brown. Drain. Serve hot.

Filling

$1/2$ kg potatoes	4 tsps coarse coriander
3 tsps white cuminseeds	powder
1 tsp black pepper	1 tsp red chilli powder
1 tsp chopped fresh	3 green chillies
coriander leaves	60 gms boiled peas
1 tbsp ghee	salt to taste

Boil the potatoes, peel and cut into small pieces. Heat the ghee, add potatoes, spices, chopped coriander, peas and salt and cook for two minutes, cool, then fill in the samosas.

KABABS

ALMOND KABAB   *serves 8*

100 gms blanched
  almond
1³/₄ cups milk
50 gms flour
2 tsps chopped coriander
  leaves
1 tsp cumin powder
¹/₄ tsp red chilli powder
¹/₂ tsp flour for batter
salt to taste

100 gms fresh
  breadcrumbs
4 tsps butter
1 small onion, chopped
4 green chillies
2 tsps chopped mint leaves
dry breadcrumbs for
  coating
ghee for deep frying

Grind blanched almonds finely. Fry the chopped
onion and green chillies until light brown. Boil the
milk with butter and add sifted flour and stir it over
the fire until it leaves the sides and bottom of the
vessel. Now add almonds, fried onion and green
chillies, fresh breadcrumbs, cumin powder, salt,
coriander leaves and red chilli powder and mix it over
the fire. Remove from the fire, spread it on a plate and
chill. Make into cutlet shapes, dip in thin flour batter
and roll in breadcrumbs. Fry until nicely browned.
Drain on paper. Sprinkle with chopped mint leaves
and serve hot with tomato ketchup. (Flour batter
should be thin and thoroughly beaten like pakora
batter).

CASHEWNUT KABAB

serves 8

Follow the above recipe except omit almonds and add coarsely ground cashewnuts, instead.

DAL KABAB

serves 8

250 gms chana dal
1 tbsp milk
1 tsp chopped coriander
   leaves
2 tsps chopped green
   chillies
$^1/_4$ tsp red chilli powder
ghee for frying

$^1/_2$ kg boiled potatoes
1 tsp chopped ginger
1 tsp chopped onion
$^1/_4$ tsp black pepper
2 tsps ground spices
breadcrumbs for coating
30 gms flour for batter

Pick and wash the chana dal and boil in salt water until tender. Put in a strainer to remove excess water. Grate the boiled potatoes in it, mix milk, salt and black pepper. Mix chopped ingredients, salt and red chilli powder with boiled dal. Take a ball of the potato mixture and make a depression in the centre, fill with the dal mixture. Now cover with more of the potato mixture. Flatten and shape into round cakes 5 cms in diameter. Dip into flour batter and roll in breadcrumbs. Fry in hot ghee until golden brown and drain on paper. Serve hot with mint chutney or tomato ketchup.

ENERGY KABAB

serves 8

1 turnip
2 carrots
1 boiled potato
$^1/_4$ tsp black pepper
1 tsp chopped coriander
   leaves

120 gms peas
120 gms beans
2 green chillies
$^1/_2$ small onion
3 tsps dry breadcrumbs
6 tsps flour

$^1/_4$ tsp red chilli powder
$^1/_2$ tsp chopped ginger
3 tsps ghee
4 tsps whipped cream
80 gms butter

ghee to fry breadcrumbs
30 gms flour for batter
5 gms grated cheese
120 gms potatoes

Chop all the vegetables and steam until tender. Fry chopped onion, green chillies and ginger in 1 tbsp ghee until light brown. Add the flour and fry for one minute, then put in steamed vegetables, salt, pepper and cook for 2 minutes. Chill and then add 3 tsps dry breadcrumbs and mix well. Make a paste of butter, grated cheese, whipped cream and chill. Make balls of this chilled paste and cover with vegetables and then shape into round balls. Dust with flour and dip in the batter and roll in breadcrumbs. Deep fry in ghee until brown. Drain on paper. Place the energy kababs on a bed of 120 gms of boiled and mashed potatoes and serve hot.

MIXED VEGETABLE CREAM KABAB *serves 8*

2 turnips
4 carrots
2 boiled potatoes
1 small onion
2 tbsps dry breadcrumbs
2 tsps cumin powder
8 tsps flour
5 tsps butter
breadcrumbs for coating
$^1/_2$ cup flour for batter
salt to taste

250 gms peas
250 gms beans
4 green chillies
2 tsps chopped coriander
   leaves
$^1/_2$ tsp black pepper
$^1/_2$ tsp red chilli powder
1 tsp chopped ginger
$^1/_4$ cup cream
ghee to fry

Chop all the vegetables and steam or boil them. Fry chopped onion, green chillies and ginger in 1 tbsp of ghee until light brown. Add the flour and fry for one minute, then add steamed vegetables, salt, pepper, red chilli powder and ground cuminseeds and cook for 3 minutes. Chill and add 2 tbsps breadcrumbs and mix. Make a paste of whipped cream and butter and chill. Make oval-shaped cutlets and fill chilled cream in them. Dust with flour, dip in flour batter and roll in breadcrumbs. Deep fry in ghee until brown. Drain on paper and serve with tomato ketchup.

POTATO CREAM KABAB   serves 8

1 kg potatoes
30 gms butter
$1/_4$ cup whipped cream
$1/_4$ cup milk
2 to 3 green chillies
ghee for frying
$1/_2$ teacup flour for batter
$1/_3$ cup water for batter
salt to taste

$1/_2$ tsp red chilli powder
$1/_4$ tsp black pepper
2 tsps ground ginger
2 tsps chopped coriander
   leaves
breadcrumbs for coating
25 gms flour for dusting
   the rolls

Boil the potatoes, cool, mash and mix with salt, red chilli powder, black pepper, milk and melted butter, chopped green chillies and coriander leaves. Cook for 3 minutes. Remove from the fire and cool. Make a batter of the flour. Shape smooth balls of mashed potato mixture by rolling it round a spoon or between the palms of the hands. Fill the cream in the balls. Dust with flour, dip in flour batter and roll in breadcrumbs. Fry in hot ghee until brown. Drain on paper. Serve hot with curd chutney.

POTATO KABAB (PARSI) *serves 8*

750 gms potatoes
1/2 fresh coconut or one
   cup grated dry coconut
2 slices bread
3 green chillies
2 tsps ground spices
2 tsps finely chopped
   ginger
dry breadcrumbs for
   coating

1 tsp salt for boiling
   potatoes
2 tsps chopped coriander
   leaves
1/2 tsp red chilli powder
1 tsp white cuminseeds
1 medium tomato
ghee for deep frying
25 gms flour for batter

Boil the potatoes in salted water until tender. Cool and mash them. Remove the brown part of fresh coconut and grate. Soak bread slices in water and squeeze out the liquid. Heat 1 tbsp ghee and fry chopped ginger, green chillies, grated coconut until light brown. Add chopped coriander leaves, ground spices, white cuminseeds, salt, chopped tomatoes, bread slices, red chilli powder and cook until the mixture is dry. Cool the mixture. Make 12 round balls of mashed potatoes and fill each with cooked coconut. Make a batter of the flour and dip kababs in it, roll in dry breadcrumbs. Fry in hot ghee until light brown. Drain on paper and serve. (If using dry coconut, soak in 1 cup of water for 35 minutes and strain through a thin cloth.)

SEEKH KABAB *serves 8*

750 gms bhein
1 tsp ground ginger
3 tsps white cuminseeds
2 tsps chopped coriander
   leaves
1/4 tsp red chilli powder
salt to taste

1/2 onion
3 to 4 green chillies
2 tsps ground spices
100 gms roasted and
   skinned chana
ghee to fry

Scrape and cut bhein into thin slices and boil in salted water until tender. Remove from the fire and cool. Mash, add salt, ground spices, ginger, ground white cuminseeds, chopped coriander leaves, onion, green chillies, red chilli powder, and powdered chana and mix well. Put the mixture round an iron rod and grill on a charcoal fire or in an oven until light brown in colour. Heat one tbsp ghee well in a frying pan, and fry seekh kabab until brown.

SEMOLINA KABAB   serves 8

120 gms semolina
4 tsps butter
$1/_2$ tsp red chilli powder
3 tsps tomato ketchup
1 tsp ground spices
$1/_2$ cup flour for batter
a few green coriander
   leaves

3 cups milk
100 gms grated cheese
2 to 3 green chillies
2 tsps chopped ginger
ghee to fry
breadcrumbs for coating
a few mint leaves
salt to taste

Heat the milk and butter and add semolina. Cook until the mixture is thick. Remove from the fire. Add grated cheese, salt, red chilli powder, ground coriander leaves, green chillies, ginger, tomato ketchup and ground spices. Spread the mixture on a plate and chill until set. Cut into cutlet shapes; dust with flour, dip in flour batter, roll in breadcrumbs and deep fry in ghee until brown.

VEGETABLE CREAM KABAB   serves 8

1 small onion
3 tsps ginger
$1/_2$ kg peas
$1/_2$ kg beans

2 green chillies
4 turnips
250 gms carrots
250 gms boiled potatoes

1 tsp black pepper
12 tsps dry breadcrumbs
1 tsp ground spices
120 gms butter
breadcrumbs for coating
mint leaves for decoration
ghee for deep frying
salt to taste

4 tsps chopped coriander
leaves
$1/_2$ tsp red chilli powder
5 tsps flour
$1/_2$ cup cream
120 gms flour for making
batter

Chop the vegetables and boil until tender. Fry chopped onion, green chillies and ginger in 1 tbsp ghee until light brown. Add flour and fry for one minute and mix in boiled vegetables, salt, pepper, red chilli powder, ground spices and 6 tsps breadcrumbs and chill. Make a paste of whipped cream and butter and chill. Shape the vegetable mixture into pears and in it fill chilled cream. Dust with flour and then dip into flour batter and roll in breadcrumbs. Deep fry in ghee until brown. Drain on paper decorated with fresh mint leaves.

RICE KABAB   *serves 8*

120 gms ground rice
4 tsps butter
50 gms cheese
1 tsp cumin powder
$1/_4$ tsp black pepper
1 chopped green chilli
slices of one lemon
salt to taste

3 cups milk
$1/_4$ cup flour for batter
$1^1/_2$ cups breadcrumbs
$1/_2$ tsp red chilli powder
1 ground clove
1 tsp chopped coriander
leaves
a few mint leaves

Boil the milk with butter, add rice flour and stir until thick. Remove from the fire, add grated cheese, salt, pepper, red chilli powder, chopped green chillies, cloves, cuminseed powder and coriander leaves. Chill, then make into fillet shapes. Dip in flour batter and coat with breadcrumbs. Deep fry in ghee until brown. Decorate with lemon slices and mint leaves.

FRUIT CHAT   *serves 8*

Masala

3 tsps ground spices

3 tsps ground red chillies

3 tsps amchoor

$1/_4$ tsp citric acid

7 tsps cuminseeds,
    roasted and powdered

2 tsps black pepper

$1^1/_2$ tsps salt

$1^1/_2$ tsps black salt

2 tsps fine sugar

1 tsp thymol powder

Mix all the above ground
    spices together

Fruit

250 gms potatoes

1 kachalu (a variety
  of potato)

250 gms sweet potatoes

250 gms papaya

1 tomato without pulp

250 gms lemons

250 gms peas

250 gms guava

4 bananas

1 tsp salt for boiling peas
  and potatoes

Boil sweet potatoes, peas and potatoes together in salted water till tender. Boil kachalu, also in salted water, but separately. Cut all the fruit into small pieces and mix with masala and lemon juice. Sprinkle with roasted cumin powder.

INDIAN SWEETS

Halwa

ALMOND HALWA
serves 6

250 gms almond
2 silver leaves
3 cups milk
6 green cardamoms

250 gms ghee
120 gms semolina
1 cup sugar
$^1/_2$ tsp chopped pistachios

Soak almonds overnight, peel and then grind coarsely. Boil the milk with sugar until it is dissolved, and keep aside. Heat the ghee, fry semolina for two minutes, mix coarsely ground almonds and fry until light brown. Now add milk and crushed cardamoms, stir until thick and leaves its ghee. Remove from the fire, put in a serving dish and decorate with silver leaves. Sprinkle chopped pistachios over it and serve hot.

CARROT HALWA
serves 6

2 kgs carrots
4 silver leaves
$^1/_2$ kg khoya
50 gms skinned almonds
6 green cardamoms

$^1/_2$ kg sugar
1 cup water
$1^1/_2$ cups ghee
50 gms pistachios

Grate the carrots. Make one thread syrup of sugar and water. Add to it 300 gms mashed khoya and stir until well mixed. Add the grated carrots, green cardamoms and ghee and stir on a hot fire until water of carrots is absorbed. Then add 200 gms khoya, chopped almonds and pistachios and mix well. Decorate with silver leaves. Serve hot.

MOONG DAL HALWA   *serves 8*

$1/_2$ kg split moong dal	300 gms ghee
$2^1/_2$ cups milk	200 gms khoya
300 gms sugar	15 gms almonds
15 gms raisins	15 gms pistachios

Soak the moong dal in water for 6 to 8 hours. Remove the husks by rubbing in several changes of water. Then grind the dal into a fine paste. Heat the ghee and fry the paste until golden brown in colour and a very agreeable fragrance is given off. Add the milk and sugar and stir for 5 minutes, till thick and soft. Add the khoya and cook for one minute. Remove from the fire. Garnish with blanched and chopped almonds and pistachio nuts. Serve hot.

RAJ BHOG HALWA   *serves 12*

$1/_2$ kg sugar	50 gms almonds
250 gms semolina	50 gms pistachios
250 gms ghee	6 cups water
1 tbsp besan	250 gms khoya
5 big cardamoms	yellow colour
200 gms ghee	

Make a sticky syrup of sugar in water and add yellow colour. Fry the semolina in ghee until light brown, add besan, cardamoms and fry until golden brown. Pour hot syrup over the fried semolina, then add mashed khoya, peeled almonds and pistachio slices and stir for 5 minutes over fire. Pour all round it 1 tbsp of melted ghee and stir till it leaves its ghee. Remove from the fire and cover with a lid. Serve hot.

SHAHI HALWA
serves 10

200 gms suji
4¹/₂ cups milk
120 gms khoya
15 gms skinned pistachios
6 green cardamoms
¹/₄ tsp dry yellow colour

350 gms sugar
9 tsps flour
15 gms magaz
25 gms almonds
200 gms ghee

Boil the milk, add sugar and colour, and stir until sugar is dissolved. Keep aside. Heat the ghee, fry semolina and flour with cardamoms until slightly brown. Add the milk and khoya and stir until milk is absorbed. Then mix pistachios, almonds, magaz and the rest of the ghee, and stir until it leaves its ghee. Serve hot.

SUJI HALWA
serves 6

120 gms semolina
120 gms ghee
25 gms almonds
5 crushed green cardamoms

100 gms sugar
1³/₄ cup water
25 gms raisins

Dissolve the sugar in water over fire to make a thin syrup, and keep aside. Melt the ghee in a shallow pan over gentle fire, add semolina and stir until it is golden in appearance, the grains of suji swell by absorbing the ghee and a very agreeable smell is given off. Pour the thin syrup of sugar over it. Add raisins, crushed green cardamoms, blanched and chopped almonds and fry a little. Remove from the fire and serve hot.

WHEAT HALWA
serves 8

250 gms coarsely
   ground wheat
9 cups water
200 gms sugar

1 silver leaf
5¹/₂ tbsps ghee
2 tsps pistachios
8 green cardamoms

Soak the coarsely ground wheat in 3 cups of water overnight. Dissolve sugar in 5 cups of water on fire to make a thin syrup. Remove from the fire and keep aside. Heat the ghee, fry soaked wheat in it until light brown. Now add the syrup and crushed green cardamoms and stir until the syrup is absorbed. Remove from the fire. Decorate with silver leaves and chopped pistachios and serve hot.

WHITE PUMPKIN HALWA serves 8

2 kgs pumpkin
250 gms ghee
200 gms sugar

$^1/_2$ kg khoya
1 tsp lime
50 gms blanched almonds and pistachios

Peel the pumpkin. Discard the soft part of the pumpkin and grate the rest. Squeeze lime in water and soak pumpkin in it for 10 minutes. Then wash it several times in water until there is no taste of lime left. Squeeze out the water lightly. Put the ghee, grated pumpkin and khoya in a heavy pan and stir on hot fire until dry. Now add sugar and stir until it is dissolved and it leaves the sides of pan clear. Remove from the fire, put in a serving dish. Decorate with silver leaves and sprinkle chopped almonds and pistachios. Serve hot.

Kheer

CHEWRA KHEER (Pressed Rice) serves 6

1 litre buffalo milk
120 gms sugar
10 gms blanched and
   slivered almonds
6 ground green
   cardamoms

50 gms chewra
50 gms ghee
10 gms blanched and
   slivered pistachios
2 tsps kewra essence

Fry the chewra in ghee on a low fire until golden brown and then drain the fat. Boil the milk with crushed cardamoms, add fried chewra and stir until tender and milk becomes thick. Add sugar and stir until it is dissolved. Remove from the fire and mix kewra flavour. Pour in a serving dish, decorate with silver leaves and slivered almonds and pistachios. Serve lukewarm or cold.

LAUKI KHEER
serves 8

1 litre buffalo milk
100 gms sugar
4 green cardamoms

250 gms lauki
50 gms blanched almonds
    and pistachios

Boil the milk with green cardamoms, add grated lauki, and stir until thick and lauki is tender. Remove from the fire, add sugar, chopped pistachios and almonds. Serve hot or cold.

CARROT KHEER
serves 8

Substitute carrots for lauki in the above recipe.

RICE KHEER
serves 6

1 litre buffalo milk
75 gms sugar
15 gms raisins, cleaned
2 big cardamoms

50 gms rice
25 gms blanched almonds
5 gms pistachios
1 tsp kewra essence

Wash and soak the rice for 25 minutes. Boil the milk with cardamom seeds, add the rice and stir until rice is quite tender, and well mixed with milk. Remove from the fire. Add sugar, chopped almonds, pistachios and raisins. Cool and mix kewra flavour. Serve hot.

SPECIAL RICE KHEER *serves 6*

250 gms rice
100 gms sugar
50 gms khoya
25 gms raisins

1 litre buffalo milk
6 green cardamoms
25 gms blanched almonds
$1/_2$ tsp rose essence

Wash and soak the rice in water for 15 minutes. Drain and cook in milk until tender. Continue cooking until the kheer is quite thick. Add sugar, khoya, raisins, almonds, pistachios and crushed green cardamoms and mix well. Remove from the fire, cool and then mix rose flavour. Serve as dessert.

FIRNI *serves 12*

Method—1

$1/_2$ litre milk
250 gms sugar
silver leaves
50 gms pistachios
2 tsps kewra essence

100 gms cornflour
350 gms khoya
50 gms almonds
8 big cardamoms

Boil the milk with khoya until well mixed. Mix the cornflour in a little water and add to the milk and stir until thick. Remove from the fire, add sugar, kewra and mix well. Pour into 14 dessert bowls and chill until set. Decorate with silver leaves, crushed cardamoms, chopped pistachios and skinned almonds.

Method—2

120 gms rice
6 tbsps sugar
6 cups milk

50 gms pistachios
2 tsps kewra essence

Soak the rice for 4 hours, drain the water, dry it with a cloth, and grind into powder. Mix the rice powder with

1 cup of milk. Heat the rest of the milk and gradually add the milk and rice powder mixture to it. Cook on a low fire till thick, stirring all the time. Add sugar and let it dissolve. Remove from the fire and mix kewra essence in it. Serve in dessert bowls decorated with chopped pistachios, almonds and silver leaves.

SHAHI TUKRI   serves 10

12 slices bread	6 cups milk
250 gms sugar	$^1/_2$ tsp saffron
2 tsps kewra flavour	250 gms khoya
10 green cardamoms	4 silver leaves
25 gms almonds	10 gms pistachio nuts
4 cherries	ghee to fry

Remove the hard crusts of bread slices and fry in ghee till golden brown. Remove and drain. Boil the milk with crushed cardamoms and dissolve saffron and sugar in it. Soak the fried bread slices in it for a few minutes. Remove them from the milk with a flat spoon. Mix the khoya with milk and put on the fire for five minutes and then place the bread slices in it. Cook on a low fire till the mixture thickens. Turn the slices once or twice with a flat spoon. Remove from the fire and cool a little. Add kewra essence. Place them in a serving dish, decorate with silver leaves and sprinkle with chopped almonds, pistachio nuts and cherries. Serve cold.

SHAHI PUDDING   serves 6

1 litre milk	100 gms sugar
$^1/_2$ cup water	5 tsps cornflour
50 gms paneer	1 tsp kewra essence
1 tsp pistachios	1 tsp blanched almonds

83

Boil the milk and let it thicken till it is reduced to half the quantity. Mix the cornflour in water, add to the thickened milk and stir till thick. Put sugar and water on fire till a sticky syrup is formed, then add grated paneer and stir till again sticky and mix into the milk mixture. Put into a serving dish, decorate with silver leaves, sprinkle with kewra flavour, chopped pistachios and almonds and cool.

Sevian (Vermicelli)

DRY SEVIAN
serves 8

250 gms sevian
$1/2$ cup ghee
$1/4$ tsp nutmeg
5 gms pistachio nuts
50 gms raisins

$2^1/2$ cups water
250 gms sugar
10 gms blanched almond
4 silver leaves

Fry sevian in $1/2$ cup ghee till golden brown. Put water, ghee, sugar and nutmeg in a vessel, on fire. When it is at boiling point add fried sevian and cook till the water is absorbed. Then place it on very low fire, or put some live charcoal pieces on the lid of the degchi or put the vessel in a moderate oven for 10 minutes. After 3 minutes it is ready to be served.

SEVIAN IN KHEER
serves 8

120 gms sevian
$3/4$ cup sugar
$1/4$ cup raisins
a few drops rose essence

6 cups milk
3 tbsps ghee
$1/4$ cup blanched almonds

Boil the milk with ghee and sugar. Then add sevian. When sevian are tender, add raisins, blanched and chopped almonds and cook for two minutes. Remove from the fire, add rose essence and serve hot.

SEVIAN ZARDA

3 cups sevian	2 cups sugar
3 cups milk	$^1/_2$ cup khoya
2 cloves	4 cardamoms
$^1/_4$ cup pistachio	$^1/_4$ cup blanched almonds
$^3/_4$ cup ghee	$^1/_2$ tsp saffron
$1^1/_2$ tbsps kewra flavour	a few silver leaves

Heat the ghee on moderate heat. Add cardamoms and cloves, stir for a minute. Add the sevian and stir until golden brown in colour. Pour the milk, mix thoroughly and cover the vessel. Cook on a low fire till milk is absorbed. Add the khoya and sugar and mix. Again cook on low fire and place some live charcoal on the lid until dry; mix chopped almonds, pistachios, kewra flavour and soaked saffron. Decorate with silver leaves. Serve hot.

SWEET SEVIAN (PARSI)   *serves 8*

$^1/_2$ kg sevian	200 gms ghee
350 gms sugar	4 cups water
$^1/_2$ cup almonds	$^1/_2$ cup raisins
$^1/_2$ tsp ground nutmeg	1 piece mace
6 green cardamoms	

Fry raisins and peeled almonds in ghee until light brown. Remove from the ghee, add sevian in the remaining ghee and fry until brown. Add sugar and water and cook on a hot fire for 8 minutes till water is absorbed. Lower the fire, add ground nutmeg, green cardamoms and mace and mix well, then cover the vessel. Put some weight on the lid for a few minutes, until sevian is tender, then mix in fried almonds and raisins and serve hot.

KULFI   *serves 8*

4 cups milk	3 tsps cornflour
1 cup khoya	3 green cardamoms
$^1/_4$ cup chopped almonds	$^1/_4$ cup chopped pistachio
$^3/_4$ cups sugar	nuts
a few drops kewra flavouring	

Boil the milk with crushed cardamoms. Add the khoya and stir until it becomes a little thick. Blend cornflour with a little water, and mix into milk. Remove from the fire, add sugar, peeled and chopped almonds, pistachio nuts and kewra flavouring. Cool and fill in kulfi moulds. Put in the freezing chamber, to set, for 8 hours. Serve with Faluda.

FALUDA

$^1/_2$ cup arrowroot   2 cups water

Mix arrowroot with water and strain to remove any lumps. Put on fire and stir until it becomes thick. Put iced water in a pail and keep faluda machine on it. Put arrowroot mixture in it and press. Take out the faluda from the pail and put in a dish and pour $^1/_2$ cup of cold water on it. Serve faluda on top of kulfi and sprinkle with thin syrup and kewra.

Faluda Syrup

$^1/_3$ cup sugar   1 cup water
2 tsps kewra essence

Boil the sugar and water, till it becomes a little sticky. Remove from the fire, cool and mix kewra in it. Sprinkle on the faluda. (Faluda can be taken without kulfi in iced milk, sweetened with sugar and flavoured with kewra.)

MANGO KULFI
serves 8

4 cups milk   1 tsp cornflour
1 cup khoya $^3/_4$ cup thin mango slices

Boil the milk with khoya and stir until it becomes a little thick. Blend cornflour with a little water and mix with milk mixture and cook until it becomes thick. Add mango slices and sugar and cook for a few minutes until sugar is dissolved. Remove from the fire and cool. Fill in kulfi moulds and freeze. Generally time taken for freezing is 8 hours.

Ice Cream

PANEER ICE CREAM
serves 8

6 cups milk $^3/_4$ cup sugar
$^1/_2$ cup water   1 tsp cornflour
$^2/_3$ cup paneer   1 tsp kewra flavour
$^1/_4$ cup blanched almonds $^1/_4$ cup pistachios

Boil the milk until it is a little thick, then stir in cornflour mixed in $^1/_2$ cup of milk and cook for a few minutes. Put sugar and water in a pan and prepare a half-thread consistency syrup. To it add grated paneer and stir until sticky. Add the milk thickened with cornflour and stir for a few minutes. Remove from the fire, add chopped pistachios and almonds. Cool and add kewra flavour. Freeze it for 8 hours or until set.

PISTACHIO ICE CREAM
serves 8

$^1/_2$ cup pistachios   1 cup sugar
2 tbsps flour   2 cups cream
a few drops each of green   2 cups milk
     and yellow colour   a few drops vanilla essence
a few drops almond essence

Soak the pistachios in hot water for 15 minutes and peel. Grind them coarsely. Boil the milk. Make a smooth paste of flour and sugar with a little milk and stir into the remaining milk over the fire, cooking for a few minutes, till a little thick. Cool and then freeze until partly set. Now put the frozen mixture into a chilled bowl and beat with an egg beater. Add colour, essence, whipped cream and pistachios. Line a loaf tin with wax paper. Pour the mixture in it, cover and freeze until set. Time taken for freezing is 9 hours.

VANILLA ICE CREAM   serves 8

$1^1/_2$ cups milk $^3/_4$ cup sugar
$^1/_8$ tsp salt $1^1/_2$ tbsps flour
$1^1/_2$ cups cream $^1/_2$ tsp vanilla essence

Boil the milk. Make a paste of flour, sugar and salt with a little milk. Stir into the rest of the milk over a low fire and cook till thick. Cool and pour into a tin. Freeze until a little set. Put the partially frozen mixture into a bowl and beat with an egg beater. Mix colour, essence and whipped cream. Line a tin with wax paper. Pour the mixture in it and cover it to freeze until set.

VANILLA FRUIT ICE CREAM   serves 8

To the above recipe add 50 gms preserved chopped mixed fruit with whipped cream.

Sweetmeats

ALMOND AND PISTA BURFI   serves 8

250 gms khoya   120 gms fine sugar
50 gms almonds and   1 tsp kewra essence

pistachios   3 silver leaves for
                                  decoration

Stir the khoya on a low fire until it does not stick to the
fingers. Remove from the fire, add sugar and beat it
with a khurpi (flat metal spoon) for a few minutes till
lukewarm. Add pistachios and almonds and mix well.
Spread it on a greased thali and put silver leaves on
the top. Keep aside until firm. Cut into almonds or
squares.

CARROT BURFI   *serves 12*

750 gms khoya   250 gms sugar
$^1/_2$ kg carrots   silver leaves
10 green cardamoms

Wash the carrots and dry with a cloth. Scrape and
then grate them. Squeeze out the water if any. Put
sugar and grated carrots in a karahi and stir on fire
until dry and sticky. Now add the khoya and crushed
green cardamoms and stir for 5 minutes, until well
mixed. Grease a thali and spread the mixture on it
and keep it to set. Decorate with silver leaves and cut
into burfi shapes.

CHOCOLATE BURFI   *serves 8*

350 gms khoya   25 gms ghee
100 gms fine sugar   4 tsps cocoa
2 silver leaves   1 tbsp milk

Fry the khoya in ghee until dry. Add the sugar and stir
till it is dissolved. Remove from the fire. Cool a little till
thick and then spread half the khoya on a greased
thali. Now to the rest of the khoya add cocoa and mix
well (if it is too dry add milk). Spread over the khoya
mixture, cool, and then decorate with silver leaves.
When set, cut into burfi shapes.

COCONUT BURFI

$^1/_2$ kg khoya
100 gms grated coconut
few drops of red colour

250 gms castor sugar
2 tbsps water
silver leaves

Put the khoya and water in a karahi and stir for 5 minutes on fire. Then add the sugar and stir until it is dissolved and the khoya is a little dry. Remove from the fire, cool a little and mix with grated coconut. Take half the mixture and add red colour mixed with a little water. Spread white khoya on a greased thali and then pink khoya over it. Decorate with silver leaves and keep aside until set. When cool cut into burfi shapes.

MANGO BURFI

serves 12

$^1/_2$ kg khoya
1 cup mango pulp
$^1/_2$ tsp crushed green
    cardamoms
1 tsp pistachios

250 gms powdered sugar
2 big silver leaves
2 tsps blanched almonds
$^1/_2$ tsp orange colour

Add orange colour to mango pulp and cook until it is thick, put in khoya and stir for 10 minutes till a little dry. Add the powdered sugar and mix well. Remove from the fire and cool. Grease a thali or a plate and pour the mixture in it. Keep it in a cool place. When set, cut into rectangular (burfi) shapes. Decorate with silver leaves and sprinkle crushed cardamoms, chopped almonds and pistachios over it.

ORANGE KHOYA SLICES

serves 10

$^1/_2$ kg khoya
$^1/_2$ cup finely chopped
    orange peel
$^1/_8$ tsp orange colour
$^1/_2$ tsp findy choppas

125 gms castor sugar
7 tbsps milk
4 tsps melted ghee
a few drops orange essence

Chop the peels finely. Put the khoya, peel, milk and ghee in a heavy pan on fire and stir until dry. Add the sugar and orange colour and stir for two minutes. Remove from the fire, add orange essence and mix well. Cool a little and make a slab of khoya with hands and chill it, until set. Cut thin slices of khoya and serve.

KHOYA GULAB JAMUN   makes 40 pieces

For the balls

200 gms khoya	400 gms paneer
125 gms flour	125 gms castor sugar
ghee for frying	10 gms pistachios

Syrup

$^3/_4$ kg sugar $4^1/_2$ cups water
a few drops of rose essence 2 tbsps milk for cleaning
                                                    the syrup

Make syrup with water and sugar. If dirty, clean with milk. Strain through a muslin cloth and leave it to cool. Knead khoya and paneer separately till' the grains disappear and become smooth. Mix them together and knead again for about 10 minutes. Add sifted flour and knead again till well mixed. Leave the dough covered for about 20 minutes. Make small balls and press them in the centre with the thumb and fill with a little castor sugar, ground pistachios and a little chhena and make them round again. Fry in hot ghee till brown and soak in the syrup for at least one hour. Then boil till they are soft. Add rose essence and serve hot with syrup.

MALPURA

1¹/₂ litres milk
³/₄ cup milk
5 gms chopped almonds
4¹/₂ cups water
ghee for shallow frying

100 gms flour
10 gms chopped
   pistachios
750 gms sugar

Stir the milk on fire until thick (pouring consistency) and cool. Mix flour in ³/₄ cup milk and add to the thick milk. Put sugar and water on fire to form a sticky syrup. Remove from the fire. Heat ghee in a frying pan and pour the mixture a spoonful at a time and flatten it. When one side is brown turn it over and take it out immediately so that the other side does not become brown. Put in the warm syrup for a few minutes, then take out. Makes 16 to 18 puras. Put in a serving plate and sprinkle with chopped pistachios and almonds on the brown side of malpuras. Serve hot.

PRESERVED FOODS

Soft Drinks

LEMON SQUASH

1 kg lemons $6^1/_2$ cups sugar
1 tsp citric acid   3 cups water
$^1/_4$ tsp potassium metabisulphite

Extract the juice from the lemons. Dissolve the sugar in water over fire, and citric acid and boil until sticky. Remove from the fire, strain and mix the lemon juice in it. Dissolve potassium metabisulphite in a little hot water and add to the juice mixed with syrup. Pour into sterilised bottles and cork tightly. Keep for a week, before serving.

MANGO SQUASH

3 cups pulp or 1 kg   750 gms sugar
  ripe mangoes $4^1/_2$ cups water
15 gms citric acid   wax
$^1/_2$ tsp potassium metabisulphite

Wash the mangoes and wipe them dry. Extract the pulp and put in a bowl. Boil together sugar and water until sticky, strain, add powdered citric acid and mango pulp and potassium metabisulphite dissolved in a little water. Cook for 5 minutes. Fill in sterilised bottles and cork them tightly. Seal the mouth of the bottles by dipping them in melted wax. Store the bottles in a cool and dark place as light destroys the colour of the fruit. Use after one week.

ORANGE SQUASH

10-12 big oranges or
    4 cups juice
3 tsps citric acid
1 tsp orange essence
$1^1/_2$ tsp orange colour

6 cups sugar
$^1/_2$ tsp potassium
    metabisulphite
3 cups water

Make a sticky syrup of sugar and water, mix citric acid dissolved in $^1/_4$ cup hot water. Mix orange juice, essence and colour. Strain. Dissolve potassium metabisulphite in 2 tsps of hot water and then mix in orange juice mixed with the syrup. Pour into sterilised bottles and cork tightly. Store the bottles in a cool and dry place. Serve after a week.

Note: Mix $^1/_2$ tsp salt with orange juice so that it does not become bitter.

ROSE SHERBET

750 gms sugar
$^3/_4$ tsp citric acid
1 tsp rose essence

$4^1/_2$ cups water
$1^1/_2$ cochineal

Prepare the syrup with sugar and water, dissolve citric acid. Remove from the fire and strain. Cool and add cochineal and rose essence. Pout into sterilised botties and cork.

Jams

APPLE JAM

1 kg cooking apples
2 cups water

750 gms sugar
2 tsps lemon juice or
    $^1/_2$ tsp citric acid

Peel, core and slice the apples. Cook the slices in water until tender. Add sugar and lemon juice or citric

94

acid and stir on a hot fire until the jam sets when tested. Cool a little and pour into sterilised jars and cork tightly. Serve after one day.

MANGO JAM

$^1/_2$ kg half ripe mango slices
1 cup water

$^1/_2$ kg sugar
juice of $^1/_2$ lemon or
$^1/_2$ tsp citric acid

Cook mango slices in water in a deep pan until tender. Add the sugar and stir till it is dissolved. Mix citric acid, cook on a hot fire until jam sets when tested. Cool a little, pour in clean airtight jars. Use after one day.

RASPBERRY JAM

$^1/_2$ kg raspberries
400 gms sugar

2 cups water
1 lemon

Clean the fruit and cook with water on a low fire until tender, then mash. Add sugar and lemon juice and stir on a hot fire until it thickens. Put a little on a cold plate; if it sets, it is ready. Cool a little, then pour into jars and seal immediately.

APPLE JELLY

$1^1/_2$ kgs cooking apples
2 cloves
juice of half a lemon

6 cups water
sugar

Cut the apples in quarters and boil them in water with cloves till they become soft. Pass through a muslin cloth. Measure the juice and allow 350 gms sugar for each pint of juice. Heat the juice, add the sugar and lemon juice, and stir till dissolved. Boil on a hot fire

95

until the syrup sets quickly when tested on a cold plate. Cool and pour into clean and dry jars.

VINEGAR

6 cups water	2 cloves
1 tsp sugar	1 tsp salt
1 big cardamom	2 tsps caramel syrup
$1/3$ cup glacial acetic acid	1 small piece cinnamon

Boil cinnamon, cardamom, salt, sugar and cloves in water for a few minutes. Remove the whole spices and pour the liquid in a clean bottle. Add glacial acetic acid, and caramel syrup in the bottle and mix well.

Chutneys

CARROT CHUTNEY

$1/2$ kg carrot	$1/2$ tsp red chilli powder
2 tsps fresh ginger	2 cloves garlic
25 gms blanched almonds, slit into halves	50 gms raisins
	4 tsps salt
350 gms sugar	$3/4$ tsp crushed
$1^1/2$ cups vinegar	cardamoms
1 cup water	

Scrape and grate the carrots, chop garlic and cut ginger into long strips, put them in a deep pan or vessel and cook on a low fire until tender and dry. Stir frequently. Add vinegar, sugar, salt, cleaned raisins, almonds and crushed cardamoms and cook till a little thick. Pour in a clean jar and cork tightly. Serve after 2 days.

CURD CHUTNEY

125 gms curds	3 green chillies
1 tbsp ground fresh	1 tbsp amchoor
mint leaves	salt to taste

Beat the curds, grind green chillies and mint leaves finely. Mix in the curds green chillies and mint leaves paste and salt. Serve with fried snacks.

GUAVA CHUTNEY

250 gms guavas	1 cup vinegar
2 cups water	1 tsp red chilli powder
2 big cardamoms	200 gms sugar
2 tsps salt	2 tsps ginger
2 cloves garlic	25 gms raisins
10 gms peeled almonds	

Peel the guavas, cut each into four pieces and remove the seeds. Cut into thin slices and cook with long strips of ginger, garlic and water. Then add sugar, crushed cardamoms, vinegar, chilli powder, raisins and almonds and cook on a hot fire till thick. Cool and put in a jar and cork tightly. Serve it the next day.

LEMON CHUTNEY

$1/2$ kg lemons	250 gms sugar
1 tsp red chilli powder	2 tbsps salt
$1/4$ tsp ground big	$1/8$ tsp ground cloves
cardamoms	

Wash the lemons and wipe them dry. Extract the juice and add salt to it. Cut long strips of lemon skins, soak in the juice and put in a jar. Put the jar in the sun for 6 days and shake it every other day till the lemon skins are tender. Add sugar, red chilli powder, cardamoms, cloves and mix. Keep it in the sun until sugar is dissolved. This chutney can be preserved for one year if it is kept in an airtight jar.

MANGO CHUTNEY

$^1/_2$ kg green mangoes   1 cup vinegar
$^1/_2$ cup water   1 tsp chilli powder
400 gms sugar   4 tsps salt
10 gms ginger   2 cloves garlic
$^3/_4$ tsp cardamoms   50 gms raisins

Wash the mangoes and dry them. Peel and cut them into very thin and long slices. Chop garlic very fine and cut ginger into thin and long slices. Cook the mango slices, garlic and ginger in water on a low fire. When tender, add sugar, vinegar, red chilli powder, crushed cardamoms, salt and blanched almonds and stir until the chutney is thick and becomes golden. Remove from the fire, add raisins and mix well. Cool and put in an airtight jar. Store in a cool and dark place.

SWEET FRUIT CHUTNEY

125 gms whole amchoor   4 cups water
    (dry mango slices)   200 gms sugar
$^1/_2$ tsp ground spices $^1/_2$ tsp black salt
1 tsp white cumin powder   2 tsps red chilli powder
1 tsp dry ginger powder   50 gms sliced fresh
4 bananas   ginger
salt to taste   50 gms raisins

Soak whole amchoor in water overnight. Cook in the same water until tender. Cool and pass through a sieve. Add to it salt, chilli powder, white cumin powder, ground dry ginger, fresh ginger slices and black salt dissolved in a little water and mix well. Add sliced bananas and raisins soaked in water and mix.

TOMATO CHUTNEY

1 kg tomatoes	1 tsp red chilli powder
2 tsps fresh ginger	2 cloves garlic
50 gms raisins	2 tsps salt
1 onion	250 gms sugar
$3/_4$ tsp crushed big cardamoms	$1^1/_2$ cups vinegar
	10 gms blanched almonds

Put the tomatoes in boiling water for 5 minutes. Remove from the water, wipe and remove their skins and cut into small pieces. Chop the garlic, cut ginger into long, thin slices. Put tomatoes, red chilli powder, chopped garlic and ginger into a vessel and cook till tender. Stir constantly until thick. Add vinegar, sugar, cleaned raisins and crushed cardamoms and cook for 10 minutes. Remove from the fire, cool and keep in an airtight jar.

Pickles

ARBI PICKLE

$1/_2$ kg arbi	2 tsps ground methi seeds
$4^1/_2$ tsp ground spices	4 tsps ground aniseeds
3 tsps red chilli powder	3 to 4 tsps salt
$1^1/_2$ cups vinegar	2 lemons
$1^1/_2$ cups mustard	$1/_4$ tsp nutmeg
1 small piece mace	

Boil the arbi in salted water until nearly tender. Strain and cool. Peel and press a little. Fry in very hot oil until brown. Remove from the fire, add vinegar, ground spices, aniseed, red chilli powder, methi, salt, lemon juice, grated nutmeg, mace and cook till it leaves its oil. Cool and then put in an airtight jar. Serve after two days. This pickle can be kept for 15 days in summer and two months in winter.

LEMON PICKLE IN OIL

1 kg lemons
$^1/_2$ kg mustard oil
4 tsps red chilli powder
25 gms mustard seeds
50 gms methi seeds
1 tbsp salt for lime juice

25 gms salt
2 big pieces of asafoetida
$^1/_2$ kg ginger
125 gms whole fresh
  chillies
juice of two galgals or
  1 cup lemon juice

Wash and dry the lemons with a cloth. In each lemon make four cuts and pack the salt inside and rub a little salt outside also. Put them into a jar and leave them for about a fortnight and shake them every other day till tender. Heat the oil till smoky, remove from the fire, add asafoetida and when it swells up, crush it with a spoon. Add chilli powder to oil and stir till red colour appears. Remove from the fire, add mustard seeds and stir for a little while. Now stir in lemons, fresh red chillies and ginger and cook until a little tender. Roast methi seeds and grind. Now mix ground methi seeds and the juice of galgal or lime mixed with one tbsp salt. Cook for 5 minutes. Remove from the fire and pour the lemons with the juice into a clean jar and cork tightly.

MANGO PICKLE (PUNJABI)

1 kg raw mangoes
25 gms red chilli ground
50 gms aniseeds
5 gms turmeric

150 gms salt
25 gms methi seeds
2 tsps onion seeds
$2^1/_2$ cups mustard oil

Remove the stones and cut the mangoes into big pieces. Rub all the ground spices—salt, red chillies, mustard oil and turmeric on mango pieces. Put in a jar and keep it for two days in the sun and shake daily. Then pour the rest of the oil and leave for 15

100

days but not in the sun and shake it every other day. Serve after 20 days. This pickle can be kept for one to two years. Be careful to keep mango pieces covered with oil.

STUFFED SOUR MANGO PICKLE

1 kg medium raw
   mangoes
150 gms salt
2 tsps red chilli powder
4 tsps ground spices
1 tsp thymol seeds
mustard oil to cover the mangoes

100 gms ground
   mustard seeds
2 tsps onion seeds
25 gms methi seeds
25 gms aniseeds
1 tsp turmeric

Roast methi seeds, aniseed and onion seeds and grind coarsely. Wash and dry the mangoes. Slit them into 4 sections, remove the stones and keep them joined at the bottom. Mix ground spices, red chilli powder, salt, turmeric, mustard seeds together, then make a thick paste with a little oil. Fill the masala paste into the mangoes. Put stuffed mangoes in a clean jar. Pour enough oil to cover them. Cover the jar closely. Keep it in the sun for only 4 days and shake it every other day. Then keep the jar for 15 days in a room until mangoes are soft.

STUFFED RED CHILLI PICKLE

250 gms big red chillies
3 tsps red chilli powder
8 tsps salt
4 tsps mustard powder
1 cup oil
2 lemons

4 tsps methi seeds,
   roasted and powdered
8 tsps aniseed powder
6 tsps ground spices
4 tsps cumin powder
4 tsps amchoor

Remove the stem of the chillies and then the seeds from the stem side with the back of a hairpin. Wet all the ingredients with lemon juice and a little oil which has been heated and cooled. Fill the masala tightly in the chillies, pack them in a jar and over it pour heated and cooled oil. Keep for one month. Shake the jar carefully every two days.

MIXED VEGETABLE PICKLE

$2^1/_2$ kgs cauliflower, carrots and turnips (after peeling)
25 gms ground spices
50 gms mustard powder
10 gms garlic

200 gms sugar
100 gms salt
20 gms red chilli powder
25 gms ginger
1 tsp glacial acetic acid
$^1/_2$ litre mustard oil

Wash, peel and cut the vegetables (carrots into long slices, cauliflower into medium pieces, round slices of turnip in medium thickness). Blanch the vegetables in hot water for 10 to 15 minutes. Then drain out the water. Grind ginger and garlic finely and fry in 1 cup of hot oil till golden brown. Remove from the fire, add all the spices and the rest of the oil (heated and cooled) and mix well. Prepare the sugar syrup in 100 ml of water, one or two-thread consistency. Mix glacial acetic acid and syrup with the masala. Cook for 5 minutes. Add all the vegetables, cook till the oil comes out. Cool, put in a jar and keep for 10 days, before serving.

PUMPKIN PICKLE

$^1/_2$ kg pumpkin
1 tsp turmeric
2 tsps red chilli powder
1 cup mustard oil
$^1/_3$ cup salt

25 gms coarsely ground mustard seeds
2 tsps coarsely ground methi seeds

Cut pumpkin, with skin, into long slices. Immerse in hot water for 10 minutes. Put in a strainer to drain the water and cool. Mix all the ingredients with oil and coat the pumpkin pieces with it. Put in a clean jar and leave it in a warm place for 3 days and shake it once daily until tender. Serve after 4 days.

ONIONS IN VINEGAR

250 gms small onions
4 cloves
1 tsp red chilli powder
2 small slices of ginger
1 tsp black pepper

1 cup vinegar
1 tsp salt
2 cloves garlic
1 dry whole red chilli

Peel the onions and keep them whole. Rub salt and red chilli powder on them and keep aside for 30 minutes. Boil vinegar with all the ingredients on a low fire for 10 minutes. Strain. Pack the onions and whole dry red chilli in a clean jar and pour the hot vinegar over. Cork immediately.

TOMATO KETCHUP

$1^1/_2$ kgs tomatoes
$1^1/_2$ cups sugar
1 cardamom
2 tsps chopped ginger
1 cup vinegar
$^1/_2$ tsp acetic acid

1 tsp chilli powder
2 cloves
1 cm piece cinnamon
4 cloves garlic
$2^1/_2$ tsps salt
$^1/_2$ tsp sodium benzoate

Wash and dry the tomatoes. Chop tomatoes, garlic and ginger and put in a vessel and cook on a low fire till tender and thick. Pass through a sieve. Add vinegar, sugar and chilli powder and cook until thick. Add acetic acid and sodium benzoate mixed in $^1/_4$ cup boiling water. Pour the ketchup in bottles and cork tightly. Serve after one week. This tomato ketchup can be kept for one year.

PUDDINGS, CAKES AND BISCUITS

Puddings

BAKED FRUIT PUDDING
serves 8

6 tsps condensed milk
1 tsp baking powder
5 tsps butter
a pinch of salt
$^1/_4$ tsp yellow colour
1 orange
$1^1/_2$ cups cream
5 gms pistachios
1 tsp strawberry essence

150 gms flour
$^1/_4$ tsp soda bicarbonate
1 cup milk
1 tsp vanilla essence
3 bananas
1 apple
50 gms castor sugar
$^1/_2$ tsp red colour

Beat together melted butter, condensed milk, colour, milk and essence. Mix sifted flour, baking powder, soda bicarbonate and salt into it. Pour into a round mould greased and dusted with flour and bake in a moderate oven (350°F) until done. Cool, then slit the cake horizontally. Whip the cream with red colour, strawberry essence and castor sugar until a little thick. Sandwich the cake with the cream and chopped fruit. Decorate the top layer of the pudding with cream and chopped pistachios. Keep aside for 15 minutes to set and serve.

SWEET CORN PUDDING
serves 8

$^1/_4$ tin condensed milk
1 tsp baking powder

150 gms flour
$^1/_4$ tsp soda bicarbonate

| 5 tsts butter | $^1/_2$ tsp vanilla essence |
| 1 cup milk | $^1/_4$ tsp yellow colour |

Beat together condensed milk, essence, yellow colour and melted butter. Sift flour, baking powder, soda bicarbonate together and mix with milk mixture. Grease a square tin and dust with flour. Pour the mixture in it. Bake in a moderate oven at 350°F till done. Cool. Cut the cake into the shape of a corncob (bhutta) and then cut the corncob into two layers.

Decoration

$1^1/_2$ cups cream	50 gms castor sugar
$^1/_2$ tsp vanilla essence	1 orange, chopped into
2 drops yellow colour	sections
2 bananas	1 drop orange essence

Whip the cream with castor sugar and vanilla essence. Spread it on the cake layers and then put chopped fruit. Mix chopped orange, orange yellow colour and orange essence with the rest of the whipped cream and use it for making corn.

Leaves

| 75 gms blanched almonds | 75 gms castor sugar |
| green colour | a little syrup |

Dry the almonds well and grind them fine with castor sugar and a little syrup. Keep a little almond paste for the stem. Add green colour to the rest of the almond paste and mix well. Roll out with a rolling pin and make leaves from it. Decorate the corncob with leaves and a stem. Keep it in a cool place before serving.

STRAWBERRY JELLY PUDDING *serves 8*

| 1 cup sugar | 1 tin cocktail fruit |
| 4 cups water | $1^1/_2$ cups cream |

5 gms china grass   1^1/$_2$ tsps red colour
1 tsp strawberry essence   2 tsps lemon juice

Soak the china grass for one hour. Boil the water, add the soaked china grass and stir until dissolved. Remove from the fire, add sugar, essence and colour and mix well. Strain and pour into a jelly mould and leave it to set. Unmould on a plate and put cocktail fruit all round it. Serve with cream.

FRUIT FLAN PUDDING   *serves 8*

150 gms flour   50 gms ghee
a pinch of salt   cold water for mixing
1 tin cocktail fruit   1 tsp arrowroot
1 cup cream   10 gms sugar
cherry for decoration   a few drops of yellow colour
a few drops of vanilla essence

Sift the flour and salt together. Rub in the ghee with fingertips until the mixture looks like fine breadcrumbs. Mix with cold water to a stiff dough. Turn on to a board and knead it lightly till it is free from cracks. Roll it out to the size required. Place over the rolling pin and put over the pie dish. Roll the rolling pin over the top of the pie dish, then trim the edges with a knife. Make leaves from the leftover dough to decorate the flan. Prick the centre of the flan to prevent it from rising and line with a piece of butter paper and put in a few dry beans or rice and bake it for 10 minutes at 425°F or until cooked. Remove the paper with beans and again put in the oven for five minutes to dry off. Cool.

To fill the flan case, strain the fruit and arrange in the flan case. Mix arrowroot with ^{1}/$_2$ cup of cold water. Heat the fruit juice and pour arrowroot mixture into it and cook until a clear sauce is formed. Add yellow colour, vanilla essence and sugar. Pour over fruit, cool and decorate with whipped cream mixed with yellow colour. Place the cherry in the centre of the flan.

FRUIT SALAD *serves 6*

1 cup sugar	4 cups water
5 gms china grass	1$^1/_2$ tsps red colour
2 tsps strawberry essence	juice of one lemon
1 tin peaches	cherry for decoration
$^1/_4$ tsp vanilla essence	1 cup cream
25 gms castor sugar	1 banana
1 orange	100 gms papaya

Soak the china grass for an hour. Boil the water, add china grass and stir until dissolved. Remove from the fire, add sugar, essence and colour and mix well. Strain. Put a tumbler in a round mould, or take a ring mould, arrange peaches decorated with a cherry, pour a little liquid china grass on peaches and keep it to set. Now pour the rest of the mixture over it and keep it to set. Unmould on a plate. Whip the cream with castor sugar and vanilla essence and mix chopped fruit and fill into the centre of the jelly. Decorate the top of the pudding with whipped cream. Serve cold.

FRUIT PUDDING *serves 10*

1$^1/_4$ litres milk	50 gms cornflour
1 tsp vanilla essence	150 gms sugar
$^1/_2$ cup cream	$^3/_4$ cup cream for
$^1/_4$ tsp salt	decoration
100 gms grapes	4 bananas
2 tsps cocoa	25 ml cream for coils
$^1/_2$ tsp yellow colour	$^1/_4$ tsp red colour
10 gms castor sugar	a few drops red colour
wax paper	

107

Mix cornflour and sugar with $^1/_2$ cup of water to a soft paste. Boil the milk, add the cornflour paste and stir until it is thick. Remove from the fire, cool, add salt, fruit, whipped cream and vanilla essence and mix well. Put in a serving dish. Whip $^3/_4$ cup cream with castor sugar. To one half add yellow colour and to the other red colour. Decorate with coloured creams using a rosette tube. Now whip 25 gms cream with cocoa and $^1/_4$ tsp red colour and make coils with it. Serve cold.

MACARONI PUDDING   *serves 10*

125 gms macaroni   1 tsp salt for boiling
150 gms sugar $4^1/_2$ cups milk
50 gms cornflour   1 tsp vanilla essence
2 tsps apple jam or jelly   1 cup cream
1 tsp red colour   1 tbsp castor sugar
wax paper

Boil water with 1 tsp of salt and then add macaroni and cook on a low fire for 15 minutes or until the marcaroni is tender. Remove from the fire and drain. Rinse with cold water. Boil the milk. Mix cornflour and sugar with $^1/_2$ cup of water to a soft paste and add to the boiling milk gradually. Stir constantly until thick. Add the boiled macaroni and vanilla essence and mix well. Put in a serving dish and keep in a cool place. When the pudding is set, decorate with whipped cream using a rosette tube and make coils with jam or jelly mixed with red colour.

ORANGE BASKET PUDDING   *serves 10*

7 cups orange juice   2 cups water
  (12 oranges) $^1/_2$ tsp orange essence
2 cups sugar $^1/_4$ tsp each of green and

10 gms china grass	orange colours
4 cherries	1 cup cream
5 gms pistachios	4 tsps lemon juice

Remove half the rind of each orange, except that part which is attached to the stem, by a sharp knife and then scoop out the pulp. Take out the juice from the pulp. Soak the china grass for an hour, dissolve it in hot water on fire, then add sugar and stir until well mixed. Add orange juice, lemon juice and orange essence in it and strain. Divide the liquid into three parts and add one colour to each part and leave to set. Chop the china grass jelly with a wet knife and fill the orange baskets with them, adding only one colour china grass in one basket. Decorate the baskets with whipped cream, cherries and pistachios.

PEACH PUDDING   *serves 6*

10 tsps butter	50 gms brown sugar
1 tin peaches	cherries
$1/_4$ tsp yellow colour	$1/_4$ tin condensed milk
1 cup flour	1 tsp baking powder
$1/_4$ tsp soda bicarbonate	1 cup milk
$1/_4$ tsp vanilla esence	25 gms peeled almonds
1 cup cream	3 tbsps syrup from the
$1/_4$ lemon essence	peaches
a pinch of salt	

Melt half the butter in a baking dish and sprinkle brown sugar evenly over it. Fill cherries in peaches and arrange the peaches over brown sugar and sprinkle peeled and chopped almonds around them.

Beat the rest of the melted butter, milk, condensed milk, yellow colour, lemon essence, vanilla essence and syrup. Mix well sifted flour, baking powder, soda bicarbonate and salt. Pour the mixture over the fruit and bake in a moderate oven (350°F) until wooden pick comes out smoothly when pricked into the pudding. Immediately turn the pudding upside down on a serving plate. Do not remove the baking dish for a few minutes, otherwise brown sugar mixture will run down over the cake. Serve warm with cream.

RAW COCONUT PUDDING *serves 6*

2 raw coconuts
300 gms sugar
125 gms khoya
2 tsps kewra essence

3 cups milk
5 gms china grass
10 gms pistachios and almonds

Scrape off the brown layer from the coconut and break it into tiny pieces. Grind the coconut to a fine paste and strain through a clean muslin cloth to take out the coconut milk. Soak china grass for 25 minutes. Now boil together milk, coconut milk, khoya and soaked china grass on a very low fire, stirring all the time, till well blended and of a thick consistency. Remove from the fire and add sugar and kewra. Keep on the fire again for two minutes and mix thoroughly. Put in a pudding dish, garnish with finely chopped almonds and pistachio nuts and serve cold.

Cakes

ALMOND CAKE *serves 6*

2 tbsps condensed milk
$1/_4$ tsp salt
1 cup milk
$1/_4$ tsp soda bicarbonate
$1/_4$ tsp yellow colour
$1/_4$ tsp lemon essence

1 cup flour
75 gms peeled and ground almonds
1 tsp baking powder
5 tsps butter
$1/_4$ tsp almond essence

Beat the melted butter, condensed milk, milk and essence and mix with sifted flour, salt, soda and baking powder and crushed almonds. Grease a round 20 cm cake tin and dust with flour. Pour the mixture in it and bake in a hot oven (375°F). Cool and then sprinkle with icing sugar.

CHERRY CAKE   serves 8

$^1/_2$ tin condensed milk
1 cup flour
5 tsps butter
$^1/_2$ cup water
150 gms icing sugar
$^1/_4$ tsp red colour
cherries for decoration

250 gms preserved
   cherries
1 tsp baking powder
$^1/_4$ tsp soda bicarbonate
$^1/_4$ tsp strawberry essence
$1^1/_2$ tbsps warm water
a pinch of salt

Beat the condensed milk, water, melted butter and essence together. Mix in sifted flour, salt, baking powder and soda bicarbonate and mix the chopped cherries. Line a 12 cm round cake tin with greased brown paper and pour the mixture into it. Bake in a moderate oven (350°F) for about 35 minutes until done. Cool. Beat the icing sugar, red colour and warm water with a wooden spoon until smooth. If it is too thick, put the bowl over a pan of hot water to soften the icing sugar slightly. Pour it over the cake and keep it until set. Decorate with cherry pieces.

CHOCOLATE WAFERS CAKE   serves 12

1 tin condensed milk
   (400 gms)
2 tsps baking powder
120 gms butter
1 tsp vanilla essence

2 cups flour
$^1/_2$ tsp soda bicarbonate
1 cup water
50 gms cocoa
a pinch of salt

111

Sift together the dry ingredients. Beat the milk, melted butter, water and vanilla essence. Mix in sifted dry ingredients. Grease a 15 cm square cake tin and dust with flour. Pour the mixture in it and bake in a moderate oven (350°F) for 35 minutes or till it is done. Remove from the oven and cool. Cut two slices from the cake to make crumbs. Cut the cake into two layers and sandwich with chocolate cream.

Chocolate cream

200 gms butter
5 tsps cocoa

100 gms castor sugar
8 tsps cold water

Cream the butter, add cocoa, castor sugar and water and beat until smooth and creamy. Use this cream for the layers, sides and top of the cake. Coat the sides of the cake with chocolate cake crumbs.

Chocolate wafers

120 gms cooking chocolate   5 tsps ghee

Melt the chocolate over a pan of hot water, add ghee and mix. Pour it on the greased back of the tray and let it set. Remove small pieces of chocolate layer with a knife and put on the top of the cake. Sprinkle icing sugar on the chocolate wafers.

PLUM CAKE   *serves 8*

250 gms flour
2 tsps baking powder
$^1/_4$ tsp grated nutmeg
$^3/_4$ kg mixed fruit—peels,
    cherries, blanched
    almonds, raisins
$^1/_2$ tin condensed milk

$^1/_2$ tsp salt
1 tsp soda bicarbonate
120 gms butter
$^1/_2$ tbsp caramel syrup
50 gms sugar
2 cups milk

Sift the flour, salt, baking powder, soda and nutmeg together. Cream the butter and sugar, then add the sifted ingredients and mix well. Add the fruit, condensed milk, caramel syrup and milk and mix to a fairly soft consistency. Line a 15 cm cake tin with brown paper and grease it. Pour the mixture into it and bake in a moderate oven till cooked. This cake can be kept for 2 weeks.

RICH FRUIT CAKE   serves 12

120 gms candied peel	25 gms peeled almonds
50 gms raisins	25 gms cherries
100 gms sugar	120 gms butter
1 tbsp golden syrup or honey	$1/2$ tin condensed milk
	300 gms flour
$1/2$ to $3/4$ cup water	$1/2$ tsp soda bicarbonate
1 tsp baking powder	$1/4$ tsp grated nutmeg
$1/4$ tsp ground cinnamon	$1/4$ tsp ground cloves
a pinch of salt	

Cream the butter and sugar. Put the chopped fruit, golden syrup and water in a pan and bring to a boil. Remove from the fire. Cool. Sift flour, salt, baking powder, soda bicarbonate, ground cloves, nutmeg and cinnamon. Mix together the condensed milk, the creamed butter, boiled fruit and sifted dry ingredients. Line a cake tin 12 cm in diameter, with greased brown paper. Turn the mixture into the tin and bake in a moderate oven (350°F) for $3/4$ to one hour. Cool on a wire rack and then put in an airtight box. Serve after four hours.

SMALL FRUIT CAKES   serves 8

$1/4$ tin condensed milk	1 cup milk
1 cup flour	1 tsp baking powder
5 tsps butter	$1/4$ tsp soda bicarbonate
1 tsp strawberry essence	25 gms preserved petha

5 gms cherries 5 gms raisins
1/2 tsp yellow colour A pinch of salt

Beat the condensed milk, milk, melted butter, essence and yellow colour. Add the sifted flour, soda bicarbonate, salt and baking powder and mix well. Wash the fruit, dry with a cloth and dust with flour. Mix this fruit into the cake mixture. Grease 3 small square cake tins and then dust with flour. Pour the cake mixture into the cake tins and bake in a moderate oven at 350°F. Cool and keep in an airtight tin and serve with tea.

STRAWBERRY CAKE serves 8

1/2 tin condensed milk   1 cup flour
1/2 cup milk   1 tsp baking powder
1/4 tsp soda bicarbonate   5 tsps butter
1/4 tsp salt   1 tsp strawberry essence
1/4 tsp yellow colour

Beat the melted butter, milk, condensed milk, colour and essence together and mix with sifted flour, salt, soda bicarbonate and baking powder. Line a cake tin 10 cm in diameter with greased brown paper. Pour the mixture in it and bake in a moderate oven (350°F). Cool and decorate.

Butter icing

3/4 cup icing sugar   120 gms butter
100 gms blanched   strawberry essence
   almonds, roasted   a few drops red colour

Cream the butter and icing sugar until fluffy, add colour and essence. Spread it on the layers and sides of the cake. Coat the sides with almonds. Spread a little jam on top of the cake and pour the pink icing on it.

Pink icing

1 cup icing sugar
1 tsp butter
1 tbsp **water**
a few drops **red colour**

Put all the ingredients in a bowl and cook **over a pan** of hot water until they melt. Pour the **liquid** immediately over the cake and keep it to set.

White icing

15 gms butter
1 cup icing sugar

Beat the butter and icing sugar together until smooth. If thick, add a little syrup. Mix green colour in half of the white icing and decorate the cake with it.

WALNUT CHOCOLATE CAKE   *serves 8*

$^1/_3$ tin condensed milk
15 gms cocoa
$^1/_4$ tsp soda bicarbonate
$^1/_2$ tsp vanilla essence
a pinch of salt
150 gms flour
1 tsp baking powder
50 gms butter
1 cup milk

Sift the flour, cocoa, baking powder and soda. Beat the milk, melted butter, condensed milk and essence and add the sifted ingredients and mix well. Grease a 10 cm round cake tin and dust it with flour. Pour the mixture in it and bake in a moderate oven (350°F). Keep the cake in an airtight box for 4 to 6 hours. Then cut into 3 layers and sandwich with the following icings:

Butter icing

100 gms butter
$^1/_2$ tsp vanilla essence
2 tsps cocoa
$^3/_4$ cup icing sugar
$1^1/_2$ tbsps lukewarm water

Cream the butter and icing sugar together, add vanilla essence, cocoa and water and beat well until smooth.

115

Chocolate icing

1 cup icing sugar
1 tsp cocoa
1 tsp butter

2 to 3 tsps water
$^3/_4$ cup walnuts, coarsely
  ground

Put all the ingredients in a bowl and stir over a pan of hot water until they mix. Pour the liquid over the cake and keep aside to set. Coat the sides with walnuts.

Yellow icing

$^3/_4$ cup icing sugar
a few drops of yellow colour

25 gms butter

Mix all the ingredients well.

CHOCOLATE CAKE   *serves 8*

$^1/_2$ tin condensed milk
1 tsp baking powder
50 gms butter
$^1/_2$ tsp vanilla essence
a pinch of salt

125 gms flour
$^1/_4$ tsp soda bicarbonate
$^1/_2$ cup water
10 gms cocoa

Sift all the dry ingredients. Beat the milk, melted butter, water and vanilla essence. Mix in the sifted ingredients. Grease a square 8 cm cake tin and dust it with flour. Pour the mixture in it and bake in a moderate oven (350°F). Remove from the oven and cool. Cut one slice from the cake for cake crumbs. Cut the cake into two layers and then sandwich with chocolate butter icing.

Chocolate butter icing

100 gms butter
4 tsps cocoa

50 gms castor sugar
4 tsps cold water

Cream the butter, add cocoa, castor sugar and water and beat until fluffy. Use this cream for the layers and sides of the cake. Coat the sides with chocolate cake crumbs.

Chocolate icing

| 150 gms icing sugar | 10 gms cocoa |
| 2 tbsps water | 1 tsp butter |

Mix the cocoa powder with water and cook for two minutes over a pan of hot water. Cool and mix with sifted icing sugar, butter and beat it until smooth. Pour over the cake and leave it to set for 3 hours.

Decoration

6 tbsps icing sugar	25 gms butter
3 tsps cocoa	a little water
cherry for decoration	

Mix all the dry ingredients together, beat until smooth. If the icing is hard, put on low heat to make it soft. Decorate the cake with it.

COCONUT CAKES   serves 16

$^1/_4$ tin condensed milk	1 cup flour
2 tsps sugar	75 gms grated coconut
$^3/_4$ cup milk	1 tsp baking powder
$^1/_4$ tsp soda bicarbonate	6 tsps butter
$^1/_4$ tsp yellow colour	$^1/_2$ tsp vanilla essence
cherries for decoration	

Beat the melted butter, colour, essence, condensed milk and milk together and mix in the sifted flour, soda bicarbonate, baking powder, sugar and 25 gms coconut. Fill this mixture in greased and floured pastry moulds, and bake in hot oven (400°F) until done. Cool and spread any jam and sprinkle with golden browned coconut. (Put rest of the coconut in the oven till golden brown). Place a cherry in the centre of each pastry.

117

FRUIT CAKES serves 10

$^1/_4$ tin condensed milk
1$^1/_2$ cups cream
3 slices preserved
   pineapple
$^1/_2$ cup pineapple syrup
$^1/_2$ tsp vanilla essence
cherries

1 cup flour
1 tsp baking powder
$^1/_4$ tsp soda bicarbonate
5 tsps butter
1 cup milk
$^1/_3$ cup castor sugar

Beat the condensed milk, essence, and melted butter together and mix with sifted flour, baking powder and soda bicarbonate. Grease a square cake tin and dust with flour. Pour the mixture in it and bake in a moderate oven (350°F) until done. Cool and cut into two layers. Cut into 3 long pieces vertically. Whip the cream with castor sugar until a little thick. First sprinkle pineapple syrup on each cake piece and then spread whipped cream and on it chopped pineapple and again cream and sandwich with another cake piece. Lastly, decorate the pastry with cherry pieces and the rest of the cream.

Biscuits

CHERRY BISCUITS serves 8

$^3/_4$ cup flour
5 tsps butter
1 tbsp milk
$^1/_2$ tsp vanilla essence

$^1/_4$ tsp salt
5 tsps ghee
$^1/_2$ cup fine sugar
cherries for decoration

Cream the butter, sugar and ghee, then mix with sifted flour and salt. Now add milk and vanilla essence. Put the mixture in a plastic bag or an icing bag and pipe into fancy shapes. Decorate with cherry pieces and chill until firm. Bake in a hot oven (400°F) until golden brown. Cool on a wire rack. Store in an airtight box.

COCONUT BISCUITS   serves 8

50 gms butter   50 gms chilled ghee
$^1/_2$ cup castor sugar   2 cups flour
$^1/_2$ cup grated coconut $^3/_4$ tbsp baking powder
4 tsps milk

Cream the butter, castor sugar and ghee until fluffy
and mix with sifted flour and baking powder. Now add
the milk and three-fourths of the grated coconut and
knead it. Roll it out 1 cm thick and cut with a biscuit
cutter. Brush the tops of biscuits with milk and
sprinkle with coconut. Bake in a moderate oven
(350°F) for 15 minutes until light brown in colour.
Cool.

CHOCOLATE ALMOND CRUNCH serves 8

1 cup flour $^1/_2$ tsp salt
$^1/_4$ tsp cream of tartar   100 gms ghee
1 cup fine sugar   1 cup brown sugar
2 to 3 tbsps milk $^1/_2$ tsp vanilla essence
$^1/_2$ cup peeled almonds   3 tsps cocoa
$^1/_2$ tsp soda bicarbonate

Sift the flour, soda bicarbonate, cream of tartar, cocoa
and salt. Beat the butter and sugar for 10 minutes,
then add milk and vanilla essence and beat again. Mix
in the dry sifted ingredients. If too soft, chill. Divide
the dough into small round balls, then press them
with the floured bottom of a glass. Brush them with a
little milk. Sprinkle coarsely ground almonds over
them and then press again with the bottom of a glass.
Bake in a moderately hot oven (350°F) for 10 minutes.
Cool and store in an airtight tin.

119

FANCY BISCUITS *serves 10*

$1^1/_2$ cups flour
$^1/_4$ tsp cream of tartar
100 gms ghee
1 cup brown sugar
$^1/_2$ cup blanched almonds

$^1/_2$ tsp soda bicarbonate
$^1/_2$ tsp salt
1 cup fine sugar
$3^1/_2$ tbsps milk
$^1/_2$ tsp vanilla essence

Sift the flour, soda bicarbonate, cream of tartar and salt together. Cream the ghee, sugar and brown sugar until fluffy, then mix with milk. Add the sifted ingredients, essence and $^2/_3$ almonds, coarsely. Take small bits of the dough and shape into round balls. Place them on greased baking tray 5 cm apart. Flatten to 1 cm thickness by pressing with the floured bottom of a glass. On each biscuit, place half an almond. Bake in a moderately hot oven (350°F) for 15 minutes. Cool and serve.

SALTED BISCUITS *serves 8*

50 gms butter or
   40 gms ghee
$^1/_2$ tsp thymol seeds

$^1/_2$ tsp salt
1 cup flour
5 tsps milk

Sift the flour and salt. Cream the ghee, add sifted flour and thymol seeds and mix well. Add the milk and knead it until smooth. Roll it out $^1/_2$ cm thick, cut with a small biscuit cutter. Prick the biscuits with a fork. Bake in a moderate oven until light brown. Cool and store in an airtight tin.

MAGIC COCONUT CUBES *serves 12*

1 tin condensed milk
$^1/_2$ kg bread
$^1/_2$ tsp vanilla essence

1 cup grated coconut
$^1/_2$ tsp salt
a few drops yellow colour

Trim off the crusts of the bread slices and cut into 2 cm pieces. Mix vanilla essence, colour and salt with condensed milk. Dip the bread pieces into the milk, roll in grated coconut and grill until golden brown. Serve hot.

ASSORTED RECIPES

CHEESE MACARONI (AMERICAN) *serves 8*

200 gms macaroni
2 tsps lemon juice
$^1/_2$ tsp white pepper
50 gms butter
$^1/_2$ onion

10 tsps flour
$^3/_4$ cup cream
$1^3/_4$ cups milk
$^1/_2$ cup cheese
salt to taste

Break the macaroni into small pieces and boil in salted water, until tender. Drain and rinse with cold water. Fry chopped onion and flour in butter for 1 minute, add the milk and stir till a little thick. Add lemon juice, salt, pepper and mix well and then mix boiled macaroni, a little grated cheese and cream and cook for a few minutes. Grease a pie dish, put macaroni in it and sprinkle the rest of the grated cheese on top of it. Bake in a moderate oven until cheese is golden brown. Serve hot.

STUFFED CAULIFLOWER (ITALIAN)
serves 8

1 big cauliflower
8 tsps flour
8 cherries
1 tsp salt
$^1/_2$ tsp white peppr
25 gms melted butter
cherries

1 onion
5 tsps butter
50 gms grated cheese
25 gms fresh breadcrumbs
4 tsps cream
$1^3/_4$ cups milk

Soak the whole cauliflower in salted water for one hour and then cook till tender. Fry chopped onion very lightly in butter, add the flour and cook for one minute. Now add the milk, pepper, cream and salt and stir for a few minutes. Remove from the fire. Put the cauliflower in a round pie dish. Pour the milk mixture over it, and sprinkle with grated cheese and breadcrumbs. Pour a little melted butter over it drop by drop. Bake in a moderate oven (350°F) until brown. Decorate with cherries. Serve hot.

WHITE MUSHROOMS IN CREAM (ENGLISH) *serves 6*

1 cup dry white mushrooms $1/2$ onion
5 tsps butter   2 tsps flour
2 cups milk   1 tsp salt
$1/2$ tsp white pepper $3/4$ cup cream

Soak the mushrooms overnight and boil until tender. Cut them into medium pieces. Chop the onion finely, and fry in butter until light brown. Add the flour and stir fry taking care that it does not become brown. Add the milk and stir until a little thick. Add the mushrooms and cook for a few minutes. Add the cream, salt and pepper and mix well. Remove from the fire and serve hot.

Pritam Uberoi's
Bestsellers on Indian Cookery

INDIAN COOKERY

Here are nearly a hundred and fifty recipes for delicious vegetarian and non-vegetarian dishes. The preparations include nutritious and appetising soups, cool *raitas*, mouth-watering stuffed *parathas* and snacks for all occasions—*kababs*, sandwiches and cakes, and the hot favourites, *chaat* and *dahibara*. The recipes for desserts cater to a variety of tastes—Oriental and Occidental. Some of the vegetarian preparations are the author's own innovations and should delight even the strict vegetarian.

The step-by-step instructions given for the preparation of the dishes are so simple that even a beginner can produce an excellent meal. For the more experienced cook there are recipes from the Indian states and abroad that will satisfy any lover of food.

ISBN 81 207 0018 x, 1987, 152pp, Rs. 60

NON-VEGETARIAN INDIAN COOKERY

This easy-to-folow cookery book presents a wide range of non-vegetarian recipes to the common housewife as also the lover of the culinary art. There are a number of delicious preparations given under each chapter, e.g., Pulao or Biriani, Stuffed Parathas, Curries, Chops and Tikkas, and include the author's own specialities. A complete section is devoted to recipes from abroad which include some of the most popular dishes from the West and the Continent. The comprehensive contents and a detailed glossary add to the readability of the book.

ISBN 81 207 1408 3, 1989, 228pp, Rs. 60

A COOK'S TOUR OF SOUTH INDIA

Vimla Patil

In this book Vimla Patil puts together the traditional cuisine of the peninsular southern states of India. The recipes are simplified so that even an amateur enthusiastic cook can use them successfully. The collection represents the vast variety of food and cooking styles of the states of Andhra, Karnataka, Kerala and Tamil Nadu. There is a wide spectrum of recipes from the ever popular *Dosa* and *Idli* to the exotic like *Balehannu Halwa*. There are the dishes which are prepared only on festive occasions, then the sea-food—fish, prawns and shrimps—delicately flavoured with fresh coconut and cooked in its gravy. Plantains, a speciality of the south, is cooked in a variety of ways; the cool salads—*Kusumbari, Tomato Pachadi*; the rice dishes with their aromatic spices are a gourmet's delight. A few recipes of tapioca are also included. Although the vegetables used are the same as in other parts of India, the blend of spices lends them unique flavour and taste.

A glossary of ingredients used in English, with their equivalents in the four languages, that is, Tamil, Telugu, Malayalam and Kannada will be of particular help to the user. Besides the regional names of the recipes their nearest English equivalents are given.

ISBN 81 207 0947 0, 1988, 144pp, Rs. 60

Other books on COOKERY

Punjabi Cooking
ISBN 81 207 0179 8, Rs. 60

A Cook's Tour of South India
ISBN 81 207 0947 0, Rs. 60

Non-Veg. Indian Cookery
ISBN 81 207 1408 3, Rs. 60

Indian Cooking Overseas
ISBN 81 207 1613 2, Rs. 65

Indian Cook Book
ISBN 81 207 0542 4, Rs. 60

Chinese Cookery
ISBN 81 207 0938 1, Rs. 90

Party Cuisine
ISBN 81 207 1534 9, Rs. 55

Indian Cookery
ISBN 81 207 0018 x, Rs. 60

Delights of Indian Appetizers
ISBN 81 207 1353 2, Rs. 45

Indian & Mughlai Rice Treats
ISBN 81 207 1070 3, Rs. 45

Cooking the Healthy Way
ISBN 81 207 1354 0, Rs. 45

GOURMET'S CHOICE

Cakes
ISBN 81 207 1749 x, Rs. 35

Salads
ISBN 81 207 1750 3, Rs. 35

Seafood
ISBN 81 207 1751 1, Rs. 35

Soups
ISBN 81 207 1752 x, Rs. 35

Potato Delights
ISBN 81 207 1734 1, Rs. 30

Soups
ISBN 81 207 1732 5, Rs. 30

Meat Delights
ISBN 81 207 1741 4, Rs. 30

Chocolate Delights
ISBN 81 207 1736 8, Rs. 30

Chinese Cuisine
ISBN 81 207 1733 3, Rs. 30

Desserts
ISBN 81 207 1739 2, Rs. 30

Pasta Delights
ISBN 81 207 1738 4, Rs. 30

Barbecue
ISBN 81 207 1735 x, Rs. 30

COOKING IS FUN

Cakes
ISBN 81 207 1693 0, Rs. 30

Cocktails
ISBN 81 207 1694 9, Rs. 30

Mughlai
ISBN 81 207 1692 2, Rs. 30

Salads
ISBN 81 207 1695 7, Rs. 30